BACKSLIDING

TO

HELL

Mike Peralta

DEDICATION

I dedicate this book to the Holy Spirit.

He is the One who reveals all truth

from God the Father and Jesus Christ.

TABLE OF CONTENTS

	Acknowledgments	I
1	"Once Saved Always Saved" Is <u>Not</u> Biblical	5
2	We Are Required To Warn	8
3	Doubting God's Word Is Fatal To The Soul	12
4	The Fear of The Lord	27
5	The Judgment For A "Believer" Deliberately Persisting In Sin Is Hell	40
6	Torments In Hell For Backsliders Are Worse Than For Unbelievers	51
7	Names CAN Be Erased From The Lamb's Book Of Life	77
8	Hell, Lust, and Pornography	89
9	Come Back To The Father With All Your Heart	131
10	How To Overcome Sin	137

ACKNOWLEDGMENTS

I wish to acknowledge the Holy Spirit who I
requested to guide me in the writing of this book.

INTRODUCTION

Backsliding to Hell

A Message To Those Who Keep On Sinning.

"Should You Not Fear Me?" Declares The LORD.
"Should You Not Tremble In My Presence?"
- Jeremiah 5:22

God is to be greatly feared. The gospel is not a soft, shallow thing. It is a solemn matter which has to do with time and eternity, life and death, eternal mercy and eternal judgment, salvation and damnation, Heaven and Hell.

Jesus said to His friends, His disciples,: "To you My friends I say: Do not be afraid of those who kill the body and after that can do no more. I will tell you Whom to fear; fear Him who, after He has killed, has the power to cast into Hell. Yes, I tell you, fear Him." - Luke 12:4-5.

If His disciples were already secure in Him why did Jesus give them this warning? I suppose you can assume that Jesus was just being polite when He used the term "My friends." But Jesus was and always is, very careful with His choice of words. In fact in John 15:14-15 Jesus reserves the term "friends" to those who are obedient and have been discipled extensively by Him., Considering that Jesus, when He was on earth, taught and gave this warning to His original disciples face to face, how much more should we take this as a very serious warning from Jesus. For Jesus never speaks idle or inaccurate words.

The "Once Saved Always Saved" doctrinal controversy has been around for many years. I will not go into its history. That is not the intent of this book. The intent of this book is to make an appeal to you, who in the past, truly repented and received Jesus as your

Lord and Savior, but with time have now gone back into a sinful lifestyle.

To those who are back into the mire of sin, I wish I could get across to you the extreme and eternal danger you are in. As I write this I am in tears about you and all the other people who are being damned to an eternity in Hell because of the "Once Saved Always Saved" doctrine. I realize you are currently in your sins because you don't believe this way. But I hope you read all of this book before you pass judgment on what I have to say. Again the purpose here is not to win an argument but rather to help you understand and turn away from sin. Perhaps you have not thought about it much, but your sin, even your secret sins, has repercussions on those who have never known Christ - especially your family and friends. They see your sinful life and so are kept out of God's kingdom by your sin. Many of those people will be damned eternally in Hell because of your sinful life. If your life is to be light, but your light is darkness, how great is that darkness. Matthew 6:23.

CHAPTER 1

"ONCE SAVED ALWAYS SAVED" IS <u>NOT</u> BIBLICAL

Once Saved Always Saved:
A Doctrine That Damns People To Hell.

In spite of very strong Scriptures against it, the claim of the "Once Saved Always Saved" doctrine is the belief that: "Once saved by an initial commitment to Jesus, a person can never lose their salvation regardless of how sinful they live after their initial commitment." By looking carefully at the Bible, and if one believes the Scriptures one will be able to see that this belief is false.

The words "Once Saved Always Saved" are not found in the Bible. Nor is there anything like them. In fact, there are many Scriptural passages that strongly oppose the "Once Saved Always Saved" concept. Hebrews 10:26-31, 2 Peter 2:20-21, Ezekiel 18:24-32, Ezekiel 33:12-13, John 15:6, Revelation 3:5, Exodus 32:30-31, Genesis 3:1-6, 1 John 2:3-4, 1 John 3:7-8, 1 John 3:10, Luke 15:11-32, Luke 12:42-46, Titus 1:16, and many others.

I also realize there are many Scriptures that provide an assurance of salvation for those who are IN Christ Jesus. These Scriptures are also true and to be believed and cherished. Now, I hope you notice how I capitalized the word IN. For it is only those who remain IN Christ Jesus that are provided the assurance of salvation. As I will later explain, those who lose their salvation, lose it because, by their deliberate sinful lifestyle, they have separated themselves from Jesus and so can no longer be considered to be IN Christ Jesus anymore. Jesus Himself says in John 15:6 that, "If anyone does not remain IN Me, he is like a branch that is thrown away and withers; such branches are picked up, thrown into the fire and burned." Please notice here that Jesus is referring to branches that did not

REMAIN IN Him and so the branches are referring to true believers that were once IN Him but who later separated from Jesus. Remember sin always separates you from God. Ever since Adam and Eve we know this. Sin indeed separates you from God. All of the Bible from Genesis to Revelation reveals this. Isaiah 59:2 expresses this very thing:

"But your iniquities have separated you from your God; your sins have hidden His face from you, so that He will not hear." Isaiah 59:2.

Notice also 1 John 2:5b-6 which states that: "This is how we know we are IN Him: Whoever claims to live IN Him must walk as Jesus did." and 1 John 3:24a, "Those who obey His commands live IN Him, and He IN them." Notice also 1 John 3:10, which states that: "This is how we know who the children of God are and who the children of the devil are: Anyone who does not do what is right is not a child of God."

In other words, according to the Bible, you cannot be considered to be IN Christ Jesus or a child of God if you are being disobedient and are living in a deliberate sinful lifestyle. "Anyone who does not do what is right is not a child of God." 1 John 3:10b.

With this in mind, I pray that those who believe the "Once Saved Always Saved" doctrine will completely and carefully read this book with an open heart and an open mind. Above all, I urge every reader to check and truly believe each Scripture presented as written – and then check the context that the Scriptures are quoted in by prayerfully reading at least ten verses before and ten verses after. And please pray to God to open your eyes to see the truth about this subject. The consequences to getting this wrong are eternal. I realize that if you are in sin, that your flesh will not want to pray - for you know in your heart that you are guilty. Ask the Lord to show you the vileness and ugliness of your sins. Ask Him to impart the fear of God into your heart.

In spite of your sins, God wants you back but He cannot accept you back unless you repent, renounce and stop your sinning. If you repent, God the Father will happily and joyfully accept you back just like the story of the prodigal son. But you must repent. Remember in the prodigal son story the father was waiting patiently and compassionately for his son to return back. I am sure he probably looked out several times a day to see if his son was returning. That is why he saw his son returning even when his son was far off. Oh, how God the Father loves you and desires so greatly for you to return to Him. Why continue to hurt Him so? Please come back to Him with all your heart. If you really want to turn away from all your sins and come back to the Father please read all this book with a believing heart.

I have prayed and prayed as I was writing this book that every word and phrase be inspired from the Holy Spirit. The whole intention of this is so that you are reconciled back to the Father and you will be blessed again with the joy of His salvation. The same joy you felt when you first came to Christ. If you believe, you will be able to repent and overcome all sin and then you will truly have an assurance in your heart because you will truly sense God's presence in your life again. Remember, "Blessed are the pure in heart, for they will see God." Matthew 5:8. I know sin has had a very destructive way in you with respect to your walk with God. You don't sense Him any more. You don't have His presence anymore. The reason is, because your sin has separated you from your God, Isaiah 59:2. Your sin has grieved the Holy Spirit. I know the Holy Spirit has spoken to you, telling you: "I love you, return back to Me, as My child. Let go of your sins." His voice is so soft. He will not force you to repent, for He has given you a free will.

CHAPTER 2

WE ARE REQUIRED TO WARN

Message To Apostles, Prophets, Evangelists, Pastors, And Teachers.

Even though this subject may seem to be a subject to be avoided, because of its controversial nature, it is vitally essential that the truth about this be dealt with earnestly and seriously. Why? Because precious eternal souls are hanging in the balance. If people believe and live by a false doctrine concerning salvation or its possible loss, they could end up in a Hell full of fire, brimstone and torments.

To those apostles, prophets, evangelists, pastors, and teachers that would rather avoid this subject altogether, consider 1 Timothy 4:16 which states that: "Watch your life and doctrine closely. Persevere in them, because if you do, you will save both yourself and your hearers." Also recall what the Lord said through Paul, 2 Corinthians 10:5, let us "take captive every thought to make it obedient to Christ." Even if the leaders of the true body of Christ avoid this subject because of the fear of controversy, which is really just the fear of man, the demons of deception will not let up on their deception of scores of believers.

Even though many pastors and teachers know in their hearts that the "Once Saved Always Saved" doctrine is not right they avoid preaching against it in the name of unity. They don't want to offend other leaders in the church that, incorrectly, believe in the "Once Saved Always Saved" doctrine. But you must realize there is no real unity unless the unity is with Jesus and the truth. Unity apart from Jesus and His Word is called rebellion. For example, when Jesus was on earth, those sitting in the seat of Moses - the Pharisees and the experts of the law - were all in unity against Jesus. So we see that unity for unity's sake is dangerous and in fact detestable if it is not unity with and in Jesus. Remember also the unity that man tried to accomplish, separate from God, in the tower of Babel.

The type of unity that God wants us to embrace is one where we all believe and obey Jesus, and lovingly teach the truth of God's Word. And remember presenting a warning should always be done because of love for those in danger. If you truly love those who are backslidden you will warn them in accordance with God's Word.

Some brothers and sisters in the Lord may disagree with you greatly, but you must not forsake the truth of God's Word. This is not to say that one should name names and publicly condemn others who disagree with the truth as you have learned it. Rather as a good and faithful ambassador of Christ, present the truth that Jesus has taught you without malice or rancor. People may oppose you, but be faithful to Jesus. In the end, many of those who oppose you will be won over because of your obedience and faithfulness to Christ.

Of more immediate urgency, is the destruction that the "Once Saved Always Saved" doctrine has had on weak believers - causing them to fall and keeping them separated from Christ. This is the most urgent reason, that as a leader, you must warn and correct God's people about the falseness of the "Once Saved Always Saved" doctrine and about the eternal destructiveness of sin.

To see how destructive this doctrine really is, reflect on the following testimony a concerned mother had about the devastation that the "Once Saved Always Saved" doctrine is having on her four oldest children.

"When I first came to the Lord 30 years ago, we got into an independent Baptist Church which, of course, taught eternal security, Once Saved Always Saved. Now my four oldest children believe it doesn't matter how they live. They seem to find no problem in drunkenness and fornication, etc. My eldest daughter, 31, tells me that I cannot be telling them or anyone they are doing wrong because I'm not to judge. I do know I am to warn and how can a loving, caring parent not want to warn the off-spring of the dangerous lives I see them living?", Testimony From: Evangelical Outreach, P.O. Box 265, Washington, PA 15301.

Her four oldest children are only four of multitudes that have been spiritually hurt, and even eternally damned, by the venomous teaching of the "Once Saved Always Saved" doctrine. There is extreme, eternal harm in this doctrine. This is not about arguing fine points of theology. Real people are going to the real Hell as a direct result of this deceptive doctrine. Truly, this teaching needs to be openly refuted as never before. Please pray for these deceived ones to repent before it's too late.

According to Ezekiel 3:17-20 the Lord will hold us, leaders and lay people alike, accountable for the blood of those fallen believers that we had opportunity to warn but didn't. Because of this, to the leaders of the church I submit the following Biblical command from the Lord:

"Son of man, I have made thee a watchman unto the house of Israel: therefore hear the word at My mouth, and give them warning from Me. When a righteous man doth turn from his righteousness, and commit iniquity, and I lay a stumbling-block before him, he shall die: BECAUSE THOU HAST NOT GIVEN HIM WARNING, he shall die in his sin, and his righteousness which he hath done shall not be remembered; BUT HIS BLOOD I WILL REQUIRE AT THINE HAND." Ezekiel 3:17,20 KJV.

Dear leaders of the church. God has given you much influence among believers. He did this specifically and primarily, so that you could warn and protect God's people. I not only urge you, but I beg you, for the sake of our weak and prodigal brothers and sisters, that you please study and pray and fast concerning this subject until you get a revelation and impartation from the Holy Spirit concerning this subject. After this, when the Lord directs you to devote yourself to preaching the truth about this subject, recognize that satan will attack you even through those believers around you. Remember how even Peter, the Lord's chosen apostle, tried to dissuade Jesus from the sacrifice that the Father had willed for Him.

It is guaranteed that you will suffer reproach. As 1 Timothy 4:10, KJV, says "For therefore we both labour and suffer reproach, because we trust in the living God."

When you earnestly start trusting in God's Word alone and not those prevailing doctrines that are not based on the full counsel of God's Word, then you can expect a great deal of opposition. And the opposition will come from people and leaders inside the church. Even some of your closest friends and family will end up opposing you. When this happens, there is no if about it, it will happen, don't fall into hate, resentment, bitterness, etc. with them. Rather pray and love and teach the truth - don't succumb to the fear of man. This will be a hard but worthwhile road. And as the Lord directs you to do it, you will end up saving "both yourself and your hearers." 1 Timothy 4:16.

CHAPTER 3

DOUBTING GOD'S WORD
IS FATAL TO THE SOUL

It was a **lack of faith** that was the first step that Eve took when she decided to doubt God and then, thereafter, disobey Him by eating of the forbidden fruit. Recall that satan told Eve that she would **not** die if she ate of the fruit, whereas God told her she **would** die. Notice that Eve chose to doubt God's explicit Word and instead chose to believe satan. Let us read what God told Adam and Eve:

Genesis 2:15-17. **"The LORD God took the man and put him in the Garden of Eden to work it and take care of it. And the LORD God commanded the man, 'You are free to eat from any tree in the garden; but you must not eat from the tree of the knowledge of good and evil, for when you eat of it you will surely die.' "**

Please take very special note of the phrase that God gave Adam, "you must not eat from the tree of the knowledge of good and evil, for when you eat of it you will surely die." Take careful notice that the word "die" meant spiritual death and not only physical death, which also was part of the warning but not the primary part. Although it's true that part of the consequence of Adam and Eve's disobedience was their physical death the more serious consequence was their spiritual death which caused a separation between God and Adam and Eve, and all of mankind thereafter.

Let us now read where satan, the serpent, enters in to deceive Eve:

Genesis 3:1-6 **"Now the serpent was more crafty than any of the wild animals the LORD God had made. He said to the woman, "Did God really say, `You must not eat from any tree in the garden?' " The woman said to the serpent, "We may eat fruit from the trees in the garden, but God did say, `You must not eat fruit from the tree that is in the middle of the garden,**

and you must not touch it, or you will die.' " "You will not surely die," the serpent said to the woman. "For God knows that when you eat of it your eyes will be opened, and you will be like God, knowing good and evil." When the woman saw that the fruit of the tree was good for food and pleasing to the eye, and also desirable for gaining wisdom, she took some and ate it. She also gave some to her husband, who was with her, and he ate it."

The fall of all mankind, all of the sins, crimes, wickedness, murders, adulteries, immorality, violence, and all forms of evil, are a result of the sin of unbelief leading to disobedience that Adam and Eve committed against God. Again, with regard to the death that God mentioned, this death was about their spiritual death. Which in time had consequences on the physical body in the form of physical death.

As you can see, satan's trickery worked on Eve for basically three reasons:

1. Eve was disposed to accept satan's lie by the lust of her eyes "When the woman saw the fruit of the tree was good for food and pleasing to the eye",

2. She was seeking to depend on her own mind instead of faith in God's Word, "desirable for gaining wisdom," and

3. Satan was able to convince Eve that she would not surely die if she ate of the tree, "'You will not surely die,' the serpent said to the woman."

It is uncanny how satan's trickery of Eve resembles the current "Once Saved Always Saved" doctrine. Through the "Once Saved Always Saved" doctrine, satan has been able to convince many of God's people that: "You will not surely die if you indulge your sin", or "As a 'believer' you will not surely lose your salvation if you live a sinful life."

I certainly hope you see the parallel. The same tactics that satan used to deceive Eve toward sin is the same that he is using on Christians today in the form of the "Once Saved Always Saved" doctrine. Satan told Eve, in so many words, "God is easy - he won't punish you for disobeying. You can eat the fruit and indulge your lust. You won't have to pay for it!"

That was a deadly lie from Hell. And satan is using the same lie on Christians today to advance greater and greater lawlessness even among professing believers. Day after day, he's convincing multitudes of believers that they can indulge their sins without paying any great penalty - if any. It's a demonic scheme to pervert Christ's gospel of grace, turning it into a license for immorality. The situation is precisely just as Jude 1:4 says, "They are godless men, who change the grace of our God into a license for immorality and deny Jesus Christ our only Sovereign and Lord.", Jude 1:4,

Tragically today, many who profess to follow Christ, but who love to sin, are using the "Once Saved Always Saved" doctrine as a license to sin. How can we deny this? I am sure you have seen or heard about believers backsliding and committing adultery and staying in that situation, not repenting, or those who persist in sleeping around and even living with their girlfriends or boyfriends. And the worst part about it is that those who do such things still think they are in good standing with Jesus. And all because they have been led to believe that there was no way they could lose their salvation even when Scripture after Scripture tells them they are not in good standing with Jesus under such a life of sin. , Hebrews 10:26-31, 2 Peter 2:20-21, Ezekiel 18:24-32, Ezekiel 33:12-13, John 15:6, Revelations 3:5, Exodus 32:30-31, Genesis 3:1-6, Jude 1:4-5, 1 John 2:3-4, 1 John 3:7-8, 1 John 3:10, Luke 15:11-32, Luke 12:42-46, Titus 1:16, and many others.

Jude 1:4 describes the situation perfectly. The Lord has given us Scripture after Scripture warning us against falling away because of sin. We very well know that people use the "Once Saved Always Saved" as a license for immorality but we still refuse to believe that Jude 1:4 and the other Scriptures about falling away are talking about loss of salvation. What will it take for us to believe God's Word as written?

The following testimony, given by a Vietnam veteran, reveals how deceptive and destructive the "Once Saved Always Saved" doctrine really is.

The person giving this testimony explicitly mentioned the name of the "Once Saved Always Saved" teacher. I changed the teacher's name to CTA - not his real initials. I won't mention his name because at some point I hope he realizes his folly and turns to the real truth of God's Word. Before getting into the testimony I want to mention a few things about CTA. Although there are several "Once Saved Always Saved" proponents, CTA is one of its key and most popular teachers. He is a well known radio and television teacher. If I mentioned his name you would probably immediately recognize his name. He has a very wide audience and is a very well known leader in a main line Christian denomination. This particular teacher has, for the most part, many correct biblical teachings, that is why he attracts such a large following. But the one area that he is definitely dead wrong on is in his doctrine of "Once Saved Always Saved."

Because of his popularity and his otherwise respected position he is causing tremendous harm in the Christian community. Because of his teachings millions are going to be damned to Hell. Even though he may not realize it now, CTA will have the blood of millions on his hands and he will regret promoting the "Once Saved Always Saved" doctrine for eternity. I will restrict most of the exposition here to the "Once Saved Always Saved" teachings of CTA - because his teachings accurately represents the whole of the "Once Saved Always Saved" camp. The other teachers of this false doctrine seem, for the most part, to fall in with CTA's view.

Testimony by Vietnam veteran:

"I have never believed in the eternal security, Once Saved Always Saved, doctrine that is being taught today, I think it is one of the most dangerous doctrines on earth, I am a Vietnam vet and believe me when I say that I lived life to the fullest and was a firm believer in the saying 'If it feels good, do it,' but when Jesus came in, all that other stuff, sin, had to go, I cannot understand how people can say they are saved and still do the things they used to do. I couldn't, nor wanted to, I do believe you are wasting your time trying to explain your position to eternal security believers, their desire and lust for the things of this world has hardened their hearts to the truth. They really do believe that they can have it both ways - righteousness and sin.

I give this example. I have a friend at work who is a 100% believer in, CTA's, teaching, he also loaned me a copy of, CTA's, book, which I read and after reading it, am totally convinced that he is wrong, As I stated earlier, I think this doctrine is extremely dangerous. This friend of mine is married, one son, another child on the way and a girlfriend on the side that he sees several times a week. He smokes, drinks and curses. He is also one of the largest drug users and dealers in our area. This guy is always telling me that he is ready to go. Ready to meet the Lord. He even tries to witness to other people whenever he doesn't have a drug deal or a party or a girlfriend to go to. I have seen first-hand the damage that this person is doing and it sickens me, All of this because of the eternal security doctrine, It doesn't matter what I say or what Scriptures I give him. He thinks he's OK, These people love the world too much to listen to reason.", Testimony From: Evangelical Outreach, P.O. Box 265, Washington, PA 15301,

Tragically, many who came to know Christ - who at one time lived a righteous life - are succumbing to this spirit of lawlessness. They have been ensnared by this deception of satan. They have been convinced by satan's subtle but powerful lie - that "God doesn't punish for sin!"

In 2 Thessalonians 2:9-10 Paul says deception and deceivers will rise to power because people will be blinded and deceived by their own sin: "and with all deceivablenesss of unrighteousness in them that perish, because they received not the love of the truth, that they might be saved", 2 Thessalonians 2:9-10. I realize this particular verse applies to non-believers but the same principles apply to believers. When it comes to sin, God doesn't have a double standard - one for non-believers and another for believers. If anything God has a higher standard for believers.

The apostle is saying, "Those who refuse to obey or respect God's Word will fall under a powerful delusion. At first they'll wink at their sin. They'll justify it. But soon they'll actively seek out a message of easy grace. They'll invent grace that is far beyond what God intended. His grace never leads to license. It always leads to repentance!"

Many, even professing believers are under the seductive power of a satanic lie. The demonic lie that is blanketing them is a false assurance. It's the idea that they can do whatever they please with no fear of consequences. How can anyone say they are desiring and following Jesus and desiring and following sin at the same time?

It is astounding to contemplate but there are scores of professing believers who are involved in immoral relationships, sleeping with their girlfriends or boyfriends and thinking very little of how or whether it is breaking God's heart. Many others are carelessly destroying their lives and their family's lives through drugs and alcohol. People of all ages who profess Christ, and truly came to Christ at one time, are now treating God's laws casually, thinking, "What I'm doing must be okay, because I'm getting away with it."

Paul warns, "The time will come when they will not endure sound doctrine; but after their own lusts shall they heap to themselves teachers, having itching ears; and they shall turn away their ears from truth, and shall be turned unto fables, lies.", 2 Timothy 4:3-4.

Who are these deceived people that Paul is talking about? They are deceived Christians! Paul wrote this letter to the Thessalonian church - to born-again believers! He was addressing people who had truly received Jesus Christ as their Lord and Savior and had known God's truth. Yet they went back into their lusts - and now they sought out heresies that would comfort them in their sins! Those in bondage to their lustful pleasures, turned to false teachers and false doctrine to try to find peace. They ended up accepting "damnable heresies.. and many shall follow their pernicious ways, by reason of whom the way of truth shall be evil spoken of.", 2 Peter 2:1-2, And notice in this last verse that the ones promoting those "damnable heresies" were professing Christians! That is why Peter said, "by reason of whom the way of truth shall be evil spoken of."

All of Paul's messages on backsliding and deception were aimed at compromisers in the Christian community. They weren't meant for the idolaters of Rome, the heathen of Greece, or the pagan tribes in remote places. Paul's message was one of urgent importance to the church - and he wrote it to be read in churches, directly to believers!

In addition to Paul's messages about backsliding all of the book of 2 Peter, all of the book of 1 John, and all of the book of Jude are warnings about backsliding into sin. In 2 Peter 1:10, Peter tells us, "be all the more eager to make your calling and election sure." In 1 John 2:1, John explains that, "My dear children, I write this to you so that you will not sin." In Jude 1:3-4, Jude felt it urgent to tell us, "Dear friends, although I was very eager to write to you about the salvation we share, I felt I had to write and urge you to contend for the faith that was once for all entrusted to the saints." Notice very carefully that all these books were addressed to believers - to the elect, to God's dear children, to the saints - and they were all warning us against backsliding and falling away back into a sinful life-style.

I hope you are starting to understand that doubting God's word about the consequences of sin is most definitely fatal to the soul. How could it be a just thing that God would send a lost sinner, who never knew Christ, to Hell for eternity for his sins, and not send someone who came to know Jesus but went back to sinning in the same detestable way as the lost sinner? Do you really think God has a double standard? That sinning is not acceptable for the non-believer, but it is allowable for God's people? That those who are supposed to be righteous can get away with a sinful lifestyle, but that the non-believer cannot? Is this not calling evil good, and good evil? Is this not calling bitter sweet, and sweet bitter?

Paul addressing believers states: "But because of your stubbornness and your unrepentant heart, you are storing up wrath against yourself for the day of God's wrath, when his righteous judgment will be revealed. God 'will give to each person according to what he has done.' To those who by persistence in doing good seek glory, honor and immortality, He will give eternal life. But for those who are self-seeking and who reject the truth and follow evil, there will be wrath and anger. There will be trouble and distress for every human being who does evil . FOR GOD DOES NOT SHOW FAVORITISM." Romans 2:5-11.

I realize the Blood of Jesus covers us when we truly repent and live the Christian life genuinely from the heart. This is why Paul said in Romans 2:7 that, "those who by persistence in doing good seek glory, honor and immortality, He will give eternal life." Believe me, I know that it is only by being covered with the Blood of Jesus that anyone will go to Heaven, Eph 1:7. But as will be described later, there are very strong Scriptures that tell us that THE BLOOD OF JESUS DOES NOT COVER SOMEONE WHEN HE PERSISTS IN AND DELIBERATELY KEEPS ON SINNING. Hebrews 10:26-31, 2 Peter 2:20-21, Jude 1:4-5, Romans 11:17-22, etc., I realize that this is something we do not hear much, if at all, from the pulpit. But it is extremely vital that you believe God's Word about this. It really can mean the difference between you or someone you know going to Heaven or going to Hell. Sin always destroys. And when you deliberately keep on sinning you are in danger of Hell, Hebrews 10:26-31.

The reason Eve disobeyed God is because she chose to DOUBT AND NOT BELIEVE God. God told her - you shall surely die if you eat from the tree of good and evil. Instead, Eve chose to believe Satan's lie which was that she would not die if she ate from the tree of good and evil.

As Genesis 3:1 shows, satan can be very crafty. And we must

always be on guard against his schemes and deceptions. That is why Jesus instructed us to "be as shrewd as serpents, but as innocent as doves." Matthew 10:16.

It is also instructive to understand why Eve was disposed to doubt God's Word - because of the lust of the eyes. The enticement of sin and doubt work very much together. This is the situation for those who love their sin and feel they can get away with it, and not lose their salvation, because they have been led to believe that "Once Saved Always Saved." Can't you see how the "Once Saved Always Saved" doctrine is a direct attack against God's Word - casting doubt on God's first warning to man that "If you eat of it, sin, you will surely die" ?

And can't you see that any doctrine that leads to doubt of God's warnings is not of God? And can't you see that through doubt of God's warnings the way is made clear for someone who wants to sin to go ahead and indulge their lust? Can't you see that the "Once Saved Always Saved" doctrine truly is a license to sin? And lastly can't you see that any doctrine that gives a license to sin cannot possibly be a correct and godly doctrine? Do you really think that God would put forth a doctrine that encourages evil?

Those who don't seek to live in sin may end up believing the "Once Saved Always Saved" doctrine because they try to depend on their own fallible human minds "human wisdom" instead of the Holy Spirit and all of God's Word together, to make sense of God's assurance of salvation Scriptures. For they make the mistake of forsaking, that is doubting or practically rejecting, for all intents and purposes, those Scriptures that warn believers about falling away because of sin. Hebrews 10:26-31, 2 Peter 2:20-21, Revelations 3:5, Exodus 32:30-31, Genesis 3:1-6, Ezekiel 18:24-32, Ezekiel 33:12-13, John 15:6, 1 John 2:3-4, 1 John 3:7-8, 1 John 3:10, Luke 15:11-32, Luke 12:42-46, Titus 1:16, and many others.

As you can see, in the fall of Adam and Eve, man first destroyed His relationship with God through a **lack of faith**. In contrast, it is now through **faith** that man regains and remains IN relationship with

God. With this, it is now very understandable why God puts such a premium on faith - not just for your initial salvation but throughout all your life. If you believe God - which means believing His Word - then you will subsequently obey Him. If you doubt God then you will, at some point, disobey Him. In other words, if you choose to doubt God then you will get ensnared with the lies and deceptive power of the enemy.

Take as another example, the people in the city of Nineveh repenting at the preaching of Jonah. They repented because they **believed** God's warning. Let us read.

Jonah 3:4-10. "On the first day, Jonah started into the city. He proclaimed: 'Forty more days and Nineveh will be overturned.'

THE NINEVITES BELIEVED GOD. They declared a fast, and all of them, from the greatest to the least, put on sackcloth. When the news reached the king of Nineveh, he rose from his throne, took off his royal robes, covered himself with sackcloth and sat down in the dust. Then he issued a proclamation in Nineveh: 'By the decree of the king and his nobles: Do not let any man or beast, herd or flock, taste anything; do not let them eat or drink. But let man and beast be covered with sackcloth. Let everyone call urgently on God. Let them give up their evil ways and their violence. Who knows? God may yet relent and with compassion turn from his fierce anger so that we will not perish.'

When God saw what they did and how they turned from their evil ways, he had compassion and did not bring upon them the destruction he had threatened."

I wish I could write the four words in Jonah 3:5a in 100 foot letters: THE NINEVITES BELIEVED GOD! The Ninevites repented because they believed God!

But let's say that the people in Nineveh had decided NOT to believe Jonah. What if they had said to themselves, "The Lord will not destroy us. We've been carrying on this way for scores and scores of years. God will not destroy us. He is too good to destroy us."

What do you think would have happened? Almighty God most definitely would have destroyed them.

But the Ninevites **did** believe God. And because they **believed** God they subsequently **obeyed** Him and acted in the way that pleased God. Hence we see the truth of Hebrews 11:6 which says, "Without faith it is impossible to please God." From this we see that faith and obedience to God is very much intertwined.

Why am I making such a big point about having faith in God's Word? The reason is because the Scriptures that I will be presenting in the rest of this book will involve passages that you probably have either "breezed over" too quickly in the past to properly and fully understand, or that have been "explained away" and so practically rejected, for all intents and purposes, by those who promote the "Once Saved Always Saved" doctrine.

It is extremely and vitally important that you do not reject the Scriptures that warn of the dangers of falling away. All Scripture is to be believed and not to be ignored, taken lightly, or doubted. For it may be that those scriptures you ignore or doubt, or drop because other Scriptures, that you prefer, seem to contradict it, can make the difference between salvation and damnation. Those Scriptures indeed can make the difference between Heaven and Hell - either for you or someone you know. Because of this it is vital that any interpretation of Scripture must adhere to all the relevant Scriptures and not just those parts you prefer.

On the other edge of the sword, and remember it is the same sword, the assurance of salvation Scriptures are also very valuable and are to be believed as written and as they are intended. Many times people fall into sin, accept defeat, feel like they are powerless to overcome it, and don't believe that God will or has forgiven them when they validly repent. Others feel that even when they genuinely confess and repent of their sins, God will not forgive them until they perform some kind of penance or something to make up for their past sin. The Lord knowing this has included both type of Scriptures, as well as others such as forgiveness Scriptures, for example the scripture 1 John 1:9.

Remember, "All Scripture is God-breathed and is useful for teaching, rebuking, correcting and training in righteousness, so that the man of God may be thoroughly equipped for every good work.", 2 Timothy 3:16, The point here is to believe all of God's Word - especially those Scriptures you don't prefer. In fact it is probably those scriptures that you don't prefer that you are most susceptible to deception and error. It is not wise to ignore or reject any Scripture.

We must approach God's Word with an intention to **believe** fully and **obey** fully - without ignoring any Scriptures relevant to the case at hand. For spiritual truth cannot be worked out soley or even primarily through mental means. It must be worked out with faith in all of God's Word, with the assistance of the Holy Spirit, and in actual practice. You obtain the assistance of the Holy Spirit by praying earnestly for understanding of Scripture and with a true willingness to obey it., This is the only way to a right understanding of God's Word - especially those Scriptures that seemingly contradict each other. This principle is in accordance with our Lord's teaching in John 7:17 where He said, "if any man does His will, he shall know of the doctrine." The essence of our Lord's word here is that understanding follows obedience.

Therefore, when it comes to spiritual truth, the goal is to walk it out in faith rather than to just figure it out. When we do walk it out in faith, the understanding part of it will amazingly take care of itself. This is not to suggest that the study of Scripture ought to be abandoned. Rather, I'm specifically addressing the proper motive and attitude by which we are to approach our study of the Scriptures., The Scriptures are given to us to be fully believed and fully obeyed, so that we can "be thoroughly equipped for every good work." 2 Timothy 3:16-17.

With this in mind let us look at how destructive and fatal, unbelief and doubt of God's Word can be.

Jude 1:4-5. "For certain men whose condemnation was written about long ago have secretly slipped in among you. They are godless men, who change the grace of our God into a license for immorality and deny Jesus Christ our only Sovereign and Lord. Though you already know all this, I want to remind you that the Lord delivered His people out of Egypt, but later destroyed those who did not believe."

As you know, deliverance out of Egypt is symbolic for deliverance out of the evil world system into the Kingdom of God. In Jude 1:5 God saved the people. Then they believed not or entered into unbelief so He had to destroy them! God destroyed those who did not believe Him after He had saved them! "the Lord delivered His people out of Egypt, but later destroyed those who did not believe.", Jude 1:5.

Here in Jude 1:4-5 we have such a perfect description of the "Once Saved Always Saved" doctrine. It has changed the grace of God into a license for immorality. It denies Jesus Christ our only Sovereign and Lord by, for all intents and purposes, permitting disobedience without much penalty - thereby denying Christ's Lordship.

And what is the ultimate consequence of such immorality and unbelief? According to Jude 1:5 it is DESTRUCTION!, "but later DESTROYED those who did not believe", The type of destruction described in 2 Thessalonians 1:8-9 whereby "He will punish those who . DO NOT OBEY THE GOSPEL OF OUR LORD JESUS. They will be punished with everlasting DESTRUCTION, Hell, and shut out from the presence of the Lord and from the majesty of His power." The destruction being talked about in Jude 1:4-5 and 2 Thessalonians 1:8-9 is everlasting Hell!

And notice that this is being promised for those who "do not obey the gospel of our Lord Jesus" - for those who persist in their sinful ways. And notice Jude 1:4-5 is referring to those who at one time believed, remember they applied the Blood to their doorposts -

having once escaped the corruption of the world. This Scripture is much too clear for us to avoid this truth.

And notice here that the key means through which God's people went back into sin was because of **unbelief**. They didn't believe that God would destroy them for their sin.

I urge you with all my heart and soul that you please believe God's warning about sin. When God says "you will surely die and suffer everlasting destruction if you continue in sin." Believe Him! The Lord never, ever gives idle warnings. He always means precisely what He says, and He will most certainly do precisely what He says.

Don't count on the "Once Saved Always Saved" doctrine - which is a man made doctrine - to save you. The teachers who promote "Once Saved Always Saved" are not going to be there with you on the day you stand before God face-to-face on the day of judgment. Don't risk your eternal life on a doctrine that gives license to what God detests. God has never given anyone license to sin and to do evil. God hates sin with a passion. There is no way that He will allow any unclean thing or person into His Kingdom. "Nothing impure will ever enter it, nor will anyone who does what is shameful or deceitful, but only those whose names are written in the Lamb's book of life." Revelations 21:27.

And as Paul said TO BELIEVERS in Romans 11:20b-21, "Do not be arrogant, but be afraid. For if God did not spare the natural branches, He will not spare you either." Meaning that if you persist in your unbelief against God's Word and warning, by deliberately continuing in your sins, your name will be stricken out of the Lamb's book of life, as Revelations 3:5 and Exodus 32:33-34 shows. Chapter 7 of this book discusses who will be erased from the Lamb's book of life more at length., I realize this all sounds very severe but God's Word cannot be broken. The Lord truly means what He states in His Word. And He gives you these warnings so that you can come to your senses and come back to Him with all your heart.

Jesus will graciously and lovingly forgive if you truly repent. But if you don't repent He cannot forgive you. God is perfectly and eternally Holy and He will never, ever accept evil into His Kingdom. For if God were to accept evil that would mean that He Himself would be evil. And you know with all your heart and being that God is perfect and good without even a hint of darkness. "For God is light and in Him is no darkness at all." 1 John 1:5.

CHAPTER 4

THE FEAR OF THE LORD

As mentioned briefly in the beginning of this book in John 15:14-15 Jesus explained that His "friends", His disciples, were those who did what He commanded, knew his master's business, and those to whom He made known everything that He Himself had learned from His Father. "You are my friends if you do what I command. I no longer call you servants, because a servant does not know his master's business. Instead, I have called you friends, for everything that I learned from my Father I have made known to you." John 15:14-15.

Now notice very carefully, the solemn warning that Jesus gave to His friends - His disciples.

Luke 12:4-5. "To you My friends I say: Do not be afraid of those who kill the body and after that can do no more. I will tell you Whom to fear; fear Him who, after He has killed, has the power to cast into Hell. Yes, I tell you, fear Him."

Now if Jesus gave this warning to His original disciples face-to-face, of how much greater is the warning toward us? This is one area in our walk with the Lord where we have all but ignored or disregarded the dangers and consequences involved in not fearing God and taking His commandments and warnings so lightly.

For example in Acts 5:1-11, Ananias and Sapphira, did not have the fear of the Lord in their heart and because of this they figured they could lie before the Lord and get away with it. But they were stricken down. And notice this, Ananias and Sapphira were giving offerings at a much higher rate than almost all modern day Christians. They only held back part of the land they sold. In today's standard it was probably some thing like a $200,000 plot of land and where they held back about 25% for example, making the gift to be about $150,000 - which would have been a generous gift, if it had been done with integrity. In addition, they were most likely, relative to the world, law abiding and seemingly decent people. However, Ananias and Sapphira were stricken down for their hypocrisy - for pretending to give all the price of the land they sold. And notice this, their death at God's hand had a chilling effect on the rest of the church for it says in Acts 5:11, "Great fear seized the whole church and all who heard about these events." No doubt, many in the church at the time learned a very valuable lesson about God's severe judgment against sin. Make no mistake about it, GOD WILL JUDGE SIN!

In the absolute sense, Ananias and Sapphira's sin was mild compared to today's professing Christian who indulges in sinful ways. If Ananias and Sapphira's sin deserved such stern judgment how much more do those who deliberately indulge in a sinful lifestyle. If you are living a life of sin I would very much be afraid of God's judgment. You may not sense the danger now but when you die and you are present before the Lord your sinful ways will be revealed even to your own mind in full clarity of its wickedness.

I know these seem like hard words but sin is so deceptive and clouds and deadens your sensitivity to sin, that very direct words have to be used. And I would be exceedingly grateful to the Lord for His life preserving rebuke and warning. For a warning ahead of judgment is an exceedingly merciful offer on God's part. But you must take it to heart and truly repent, otherwise the only thing left is "a fearful expectation of judgment and of raging fire, Hell, that will consume the enemies of God." Hebrews 10:27.

Professing Christians, who are living in sin, are not that much different from Ananias and Sapphira. They truly do not fear God. They truly do not believe in their heart that God will send them to Hell for living in a sinful lifestyle. Ever since Adam and Eve, God has told us many times, over and over again, through His Word and through examples of judgment, "If you eat of it, evil, you will surely die." Genesis 2:15-17.

I hope you realize that the Lord truly keeps His Word - whether it is a promised blessing or a promised judgment. If God says: "If you confess and repent from your sins and turn to Me, I will be merciful and forgive you and cleanse you from all unrighteousness.", He does say this in 1 John 1:9. And if you truly repent, Father God will most definitely keep His Word. In fact it is the greatest desire in His heart to show mercy to one who repents. He will forgive you, and cleanse you, and shower you with His blessings - for He loves you greatly, to an extent much greater than anyone else can ever love you.

But the Lord has also given us a very serious and eternal warning. For Almighty God also says: "If you don't repent but rather you persist in your sins then I will come at a time you do not expect and assign you a place with the unbelievers - in Hell.", He does say this in Luke 12:42-46. And if you don't repent, then this is precisely what is going to happen to you. Remember God cannot lie. The Lord truly means what He says. Of course, if it does come to that, He will take absolutely no pleasure in bringing judgment upon you - but out of justice and righteousness He has to do so. Your sin will force His hand against you. If you refuse to repent, it will pain and grieve Him greatly to have to destroy you, but He will have to render justice. For He is a just and Holy God.

"But suppose the servant says to himself, 'My master is taking a long time in coming,' and he then begins to beat the menservants and maidservants and to eat and drink and get drunk. The master of that servant will come on a day when he does not expect him and at an hour he is not aware of. He will cut him to pieces and assign him a place with the unbelievers.' " Luke 12:45-46.

Note: Parts of the following teaching about Leviticus 10, have edited portions based on an article by John W. Ritenbaugh. (Used by permission.)

http://www.cgg.org/index.cfm/fuseaction/Audio.details/ID/479/Fear-God-Part-1.htm

Let us look at another example, in Leviticus 10, of the dangers of not fearing God. Before reading this let me explain that Nadab and Abihu were Aaron's sons and so Moses' nephews. You can be sure that both Moses and Aaron gave them careful instructions on how the sacrifices were to be offered to the Lord. They were carefully trained and given much attention and good examples both on how to live right and how to properly present the offerings to the Lord. Since Moses and Aaron saw the fearful judgments that the Lord brought on the Egyptians and the rebellious people of Israel, they most definitely made sure, as much as they were able, to warn Aaron's sons about fearing God and about seriously respecting every detail and command of the Lord.

From all this we can reasonably assume that Aaron's sons avoided the obvious detestable practices of the worldly Egyptians or the rebellious in Israel. Otherwise neither Moses or Aaron would have let them make the offering to the Lord. In spite of all their precautions, neither Moses nor Aaron knew everything that was in the heart of Aaron's sons. Relative to common human standards they were probably good boys, but they lacked a very necessary attribute for anyone who would be in the presence of the Lord - the Fear of God. Let us now read Leviticus 10, beginning in verse 1:

"And Nadab and Abihu, the sons of Aaron, took their censers and put fire therein and put incense thereon and offered strange fire before the Lord which He had commanded them not, to do. There went out fire from the Lord and devoured them, and they died before the Lord.

Then Moses said unto Aaron, 'This is it which the Lord spake' - 'I will be sanctified in them that come near Me; and before all the people, I will be glorified.' And Aaron held his peace.", Leviticus 10:1-3.

This was a very shocking thing! Aaron had to watch, apparently, as his two sons were killed instantly. Probably by two flashes of intense fire! It came flaring out of nowhere and with an intensity and heat that it consumed all their flesh and maybe turned them into cinders, I don't know.

But this happened because they disrespected God - they did not fear Him. They profaned His holy name by failing to carry out their responsibilities in the attitude and the manner He had prescribed. And I want to point out, that it didn't matter that they were Aaron's sons, or Moses' nephews. There is no respecter of persons with God. There is no partiality in His judgment. That quick, they lost their lives. What mattered was that they didn't fear God enough to give Him the honor that He deserves. God's justice struck out to leave a witness for all time. Indeed as Hebrews 10:31 says, "It is a fearful thing to fall into the hands of the living God."

Let's drop down here in Leviticus 10, and go to verses 6 and 7:

"And Moses said unto Aaron, and unto Eleazar and unto Ithamar, his sons, 'Uncover not your heads, neither rend your clothes, lest you die, and lest wrath come upon all the people; but let your brethren, the whole house of Israel, bewail the burning which the Lord has kindled. And you shall not go out from the door of the tabernacle of the congregation, lest you die, for the anointing oil of the Lord is upon you.' And they did according to the word of Moses.", Leviticus 10:6-7.

Do you know what Moses did here? He cautioned Aaron and his two remaining sons to not even mourn. Do you know why? Lest they give the impression of further disrespect by showing a questioning of God's judgment in seeking pity from God's people.

I'll tell you, Moses understood a thing or two!

"Don't you dare even weep because if you weep that will be taken by God as a sign that you don't agree with what He did."

That's pretty stern isn't it? How would you feel if it were your two sons who were burned alive? That's the side of our God that we don't like to deal with! He's showing us a side of Him so that we will understand that this fear of the Lord runs the gamut all the way from shear terror, to a loving, wonderful, reverential awe of Him! It includes the whole gamut because we need the whole gamut because otherwise we fall into sin! We don't even understand ourselves very well. And this is precisely the reason we need to have a real genuine fear of God in our hearts - so that we will not sin. As Proverb 16:6 states "the fear of the Lord makes men turn from evil."

When we see God's judgment in its full sternness our human minds are taken aback. We just don't like to believe that His judgments are real. But they truly **are** real - and they are eternal. The only reason we don't see many of them in this life is because God is so tremendously patient, not wanting anyone to perish. But make no mistake about it, when the time for judgment comes, the Lord will judge with righteousness and justice, and without partiality to anyone. For "righteousness and justice is the foundation of His throne", Psalm 97:2, also Psalm 89:14.

People have the mistaken notion that God's judgments are controlled by His emotions. Although the Lord is greatly pained and grieved when He has to judge, you must come to understand that the Lord judges according to righteousness and justice - in accordance to His unbreakable Word. This is exactly the reason why you must believe God's warnings about sin - not as men want it to be, but strictly in accordance to what God actually states in His Word. For God cannot break His Word. He simply cannot violate His Word.

Let us now look at the greatest earthly judgment in recorded history - the flood in Noah's time. Let us read.

Genesis 6:1-8. "When men began to increase in number on the earth and daughters were born to them, the sons of God saw that the daughters of men were beautiful, and they married any of them they chose. Then the LORD said, "My Spirit will not contend with man forever, for he is mortal; his days will be a hundred and twenty years."

The Nephilim were on the earth in those days - and also afterward - when the sons of God went to the daughters of men and had children by them. They were the heroes of old, men of renown.

The LORD saw how great man's wickedness on the earth had become, and that every inclination of the thoughts of his heart was only evil all the time.

The LORD was grieved that He had made man on the earth, and His heart was filled with pain. So the LORD said, "I will wipe mankind, whom I have created, from the face of the earth - men and animals, and creatures that move along the ground, and birds of the air - for I am grieved that I have made them."

But Noah found favor in the eyes of the LORD."

In contrast to the rest of humanity, Noah followed after God. In Genesis 6:9 we are told, "Noah was a righteous man, the only blameless man living on earth at the time. He consistently followed God's will and enjoyed a close relationship with Him.", New Living Version.

As you know the Lord instructed Noah to build the ark. It took Noah many years to construct the ark. No doubt many around thought he was crazy but, "Noah did everything exactly as God had commanded him.", Genesis 6:22, Then the flood came.

Genesis 7:17-24.   "For forty days the flood kept coming on the earth, and as the waters increased they lifted the ark high above the earth. The waters rose and increased greatly on the earth, and the ark floated on the surface of the water. They rose greatly on the earth, and all the high mountains under the entire heavens were covered. The waters rose and covered the mountains to a depth of more than twenty feet. EVERY LIVING THING THAT MOVED ON THE EARTH PERISHED - BIRDS, LIVESTOCK, WILD ANIMALS, ALL THE CREATURES THAT SWARM OVER THE EARTH, AND ALL MANKIND. Everything on dry land that had the breath of life in its nostrils died. EVERY LIVING THING ON THE FACE OF THE EARTH WAS WIPED OUT - MEN AND ANIMALS AND THE CREATURES THAT MOVE ALONG THE GROUND AND THE BIRDS OF THE AIR WERE WIPED FROM THE EARTH. Only Noah was left, and those with him in the ark. The waters flooded the earth for a hundred and fifty days."

When I think about the total destruction that God had to bring upon man in the flood I become terribly afraid of God's awesome judgment. Every time I contemplate the total destruction that God brought on all mankind in the flood I feel queasy and nauseous and my heart feels weak. I realize how sinful and evil we, mankind, are before God and how justified God truly would be if He so chose to destroy all of us for our rebellious sinful ways. But God keeps on giving us chances to repent and turn back to Him. But there does come a time where He stops contending with rebellious man and then His judgment comes - swiftly and surely. Almighty God did not give us an empty warning when He told us, "If you eat of it, evil, you will surely die."

God's judgments are very real and He truly should be greatly feared. Those who don't fear God are the ones who are the most in danger. They are the ones who fall into sin so casually.

I now desire to ask a very important question. But you must understand that I intend no vindictiveness or contempt against you. To the professing Christian who deliberately keeps on sinning:

IF GOD WAS WILLING TO COMPLETELY DESTROY <u>ALL</u> OF MANKIND BECAUSE OF THEIR SIN - AND NOTICE THERE WERE HUNDREDS OF MILLIONS AND PERHAPS BILLIONS OF PEOPLE - WHY WOULD YOU THINK HE WILL NOT DESTROY YOU FOR YOUR SIN?

Remember, God does not show favoritism, Acts 10:34. Also recall what we are told in Romans 11:17-22, "If some of the branches have been broken off, and you, though a wild olive shoot, have been grafted in among the others and now share in the nourishing sap from the olive root, do not boast over those branches. If you do, consider this: You do not support the root, but the root supports you. You will say then, 'Branches were broken off so that I could be grafted in.' Granted. But they were broken off because of unbelief, and you stand by faith. DO NOT BE ARROGANT, BUT BE AFRAID. FOR IF GOD DID NOT SPARE THE NATURAL BRANCHES, HE WILL NOT SPARE YOU EITHER. Consider therefore the kindness and sternness of God: sternness to those who fell, but kindness to you, provided you continue in His kindness. OTHERWISE, YOU ALSO WILL BE CUT OFF."

In Ezekiel 18:20a the Lord tells us "The soul who sins is the one who will DIE." This is the same thing that the Lord told Adam and Eve in Genesis 2:17, **"you must not eat from the tree of the knowledge of good and evil, for when you eat of it you will surely DIE."** Here the word DIE refers to spiritual death - which is separation from God.

As mentioned before, that sin separates from God is explained in Isaiah 59:2, "But your iniquities have separated you from your God; your sins have hidden His face from you, so that He will not hear." Sin indeed separates you from God. And the separation will persist forever until you repent. However, you can only repent while you are still alive physically. After you die God will not accept your repentance. For, "It is appointed unto men once to die, but after this the judgment." Hebrews 9:27.

Ephesians 2:1-2 explains that one can be spiritually DEAD even when one is physically still alive. "As for you, you were DEAD in your transgressions and sins, in which you used to live when you followed the ways of this world and of the ruler of the kingdom of the air, the spirit who is now at work in those who are disobedient.", Ephesians 2:1-2.

If a person is in such a state of spiritual DEATH when he **physically dies** then he will forever be separated from God thereafter - that is he will be condemned to Hell. Needless to say, someone who is physically alive but DEAD in transgressions and sins is in an extremely dangerous situation. He can be one day or even one hour away from the eternal torments of Hell.

All of these points are very foundational elements of the nature of sin and its consequences. In fact, you may be wondering why I am taking so many pains to explain something so basic. The reason I am carefully explaining these things from the Word of God is because some people of the "Once Saved Always Saved" doctrine say that the word DIE in Ezekiel 18:20 and other similar verses is referring to physical death and not the spiritual type of death.

But it was the same person - the Lord God Almighty - that gave us Ezekiel 18:20, "The soul who sins is the one who will DIE," as Genesis 2:17, "for when you eat of it you will surely DIE." And both the word DIE, and the context, since it regards the consequences of SIN, is the same in both verses.

That sin leads to the spiritual type of death is also explained in Romans 6:20-23.

"When you were slaves to sin, you were free from the control of righteousness. What benefit did you reap at that time from the things you are now ashamed of? Those things result in DEATH! But now that you have been set free from sin and have become slaves to God, the benefit you reap leads to holiness, and the result is eternal life. For the wages of sin is DEATH, but the gift of God is eternal life in Christ Jesus our Lord." Romans 6:20-23.

As you know Romans 6:23 is a very favorite verse used by evangelists and soul winners to explain to the lost sinner that the consequence of his sinful life is spiritual DEATH - the kind that leads to everlasting punishment in Hell. "FOR THE WAGES OF SIN IS DEATH, but the gift of God is eternal life in Christ Jesus our Lord." Romans 6:23.

Jesus also used the word DEAD to describe the spiritual separation of the prodigal son from his father. "For this son of mine was DEAD and is alive again; he was LOST and is found.' So they began to celebrate." Luke 15:24.

What is even more significant about the prodigal son is the fact that the prodigal was previously with the father. This represents the person who truly gave his life to Jesus in the past, but then went back to a life of sin and immorality. And notice that Jesus referred to him, when he was in a prodigal state, as being DEAD and being LOST. The fact that Jesus used both of the words, DEAD and LOST, clearly means that the prodigal was spiritually separated from Father God. Therefore if the prodigal would have died physically while he was in the prodigal state he most certainly would have gone to Hell. Otherwise we would have to say that the LOST can make it to Heaven - but that would contradict the whole gospel of Jesus Christ.

Jesus again repeats that the prodigal was DEAD and LOST in verse 32 when talking to his other son, "But we had to celebrate and be glad, because this brother of yours was DEAD and is alive again; he was LOST and is found." Luke 15:32.

That prior righteousness does not secure eternal life with God, when a person later persists in sin, is also explained to us in the book of Ezekiel. Again, keep firmly in mind that it is the Lord God Almighty who gave us these warnings through Ezekiel, and so the meaning of the word DIE is the same as what God gave in Genesis 2:17, "for when you eat of it you will surely DIE", and in Ezekiel 18:20a, "The soul who sins is the one who will DIE."

Listen to **and believe** what the Lord **promises** in Ezekiel 18:24-32 and 33:12-13.

"But if a righteous man turns from his righteousness and commits sin and does the same detestable things the wicked man does, will he live? None of the righteous things he has done will be remembered. Because of the unfaithfulness he is guilty of and because of the sins he has committed, he will die.

Yet you say, 'The way of the Lord is not just.' Hear, O house of Israel: Is my way unjust? Is it not your ways that are unjust?

If a righteous man turns from his righteousness and commits sin, he will die for it; because of the sin he has committed he will die. But if a wicked man turns away from the wickedness he has committed and does what is just and right, he will save his life. Because he considers all the offenses he has committed and turns away from them, he will surely live; he will not die.

Yet the house of Israel says, 'The way of the Lord is not just.' Are my ways unjust, O house of Israel? Is it not your ways that are unjust? "Therefore, O house of Israel, I will judge you, each one according to his ways, declares the Sovereign LORD. Repent! Turn away from all your offenses; then sin will not be your downfall. Rid yourselves of all the offenses you have committed, and get a new heart and a new spirit. Why will you die, O house of Israel? For I take no pleasure in the death of anyone, declares the Sovereign LORD. Repent and live!" Ezekiel 18:24-32.

Therefore, son of man, say to your countrymen, `The righteousness of the righteous man will not save him when he disobeys, and the wickedness of the wicked man will not cause him to fall when he turns from it. The righteous man, if he sins, will not be allowed to live because of his former righteousness. If I tell the righteous man that he will surely live, but then he trusts in his righteousness and does evil, none of the righteous things he has done will be remembered; HE WILL DIE FOR THE EVIL HE HAS DONE.' " Ezekiel 33:12-13.

It is true that the Blood of Jesus covers our sins if we repent from them, but Hebrews 10:26-31 states that professing believers who deliberately keep on sinning, and hence refuse to repent, are not covered by the Blood of Jesus and that they should expect eternal damnation in Hell for their persistent deliberate sinning. I realize that this is very rarely preached but this is definitely in the Word of God, as is clearly explained in the next chapter.

God takes no pleasure in destroying anyone to Hell but justice requires Him to destroy those who persist in sin. You must, you must come to believe that God is eternally and deadly serious about His warnings about sin.

"To you My friends I say: Do not be afraid of those who kill the body and after that can do no more. I will tell you Whom to fear; fear Him who, after He has killed, has the power to cast into Hell. Yes, I tell you, fear Him." Luke 12:4-5.

CHAPTER 5

THE JUDGMENT FOR A "BELIEVER"
DELIBERATELY PERSISTING IN SIN IS <u>HELL</u>

Did you know, according to Hebrews 10:26-31, that for someone who previously gave his life to Jesus, the judgment for deliberately persisting in sin is Hell? This passage is so important that it would be wise to read it 1000 times, if you have to, to get the full import of and to believe what God is saying in this passage. Actually the passage is not difficult to understand. The difficult thing for most people is to believe it. The "Once Saved Always Saved" teachers skirt around this passage and "explain it away". They come up with all sorts of elaborate reasons why "this passage does not really mean what it says." They even misapply other Scriptures to cast doubt on the passage. But we should never use one Scripture to cast doubt on another. We do not have the authority to accept one Scripture and reject another.

Remember the Word of God is a double-edged sword, Hebrews 4:12, and it cuts both ways. Believe both types of Scriptures and pray for the Lord to give you understanding so that you can see how both can be true at the same time. As mentioned in a previous chapter, it is vital that any interpretation of Scripture adhere to all the relevant Scriptures and not just those parts you prefer.

When someone, even if it is yourself, is giving you a very elaborate explanation as to why a passage of Scripture "really doesn't mean what it is saying." Throw that "elaborate explanation" out the window. That elaborate explanation, even if it comes with all sorts of fancy theological words or elaborate human reasoning, is totally unreliable because it is attacking the truth of God's Holy Word. It is better to acknowledge what God's Word is saying, AS STATED, and take it as true. Coming up with all sorts of fancy explanations and rationalizations why it can't be true is not going to change God's Word. In the end, that Word is still going to be used to judge you.

Instead of doubting God's Word, or setting it aside, or avoiding it, face up to the fact that God is not going to change that Scripture, and pray earnestly to God to help you understand what it is saying. Like I said, read it 1000 times for days and days if you have to. If your eternal life is at stake, any price is worth knowing, ahead of time, how God is going to judge you in the end.

For now let us read Hebrews 10:26-31 at least one time very carefully:

Hebrews 10:26-31. "If we deliberately keep on sinning after we have received the knowledge of the truth, no sacrifice for sins is left, but only a fearful expectation of judgment and of raging fire that will consume the enemies of God.

Anyone who rejected the law of Moses died without mercy on the testimony of two or three witnesses.

How much more severely do you think a man deserves to be punished who has trampled the Son of God under foot, who has treated as an unholy thing the Blood of the covenant that sanctified him, and who has insulted the Spirit of grace?

For we know Him who said, 'It is mine to avenge; I will repay,' and again, 'The Lord will judge His people.' It is a dreadful thing to fall into the hands of the living God." NIV.

Remarks:

First notice here that this passage is referring to those, who in the past, made a true commitment to Christ, "covenant that SANCTIFIED HIM", but now deliberately keep on sinning. Notice also that the believer who wrote Hebrews, many believe it was Paul, included himself as being subject to its warning, "If WE deliberately keep on sinning."

Also notice that Hebrews 10:26 is talking about "after we have received the knowledge of the truth" or after coming to true salvation in Christ, which is also confirmed by the phrase "covenant that

41

SANCTIFIED HIM". This clearly means, like the other Scriptures here do, that one can lose their salvation. If one goes on deliberately sinning willfully, then there is no more atoning sacrifice for those sins, "no sacrifice for sins is left". In other words if you are back willfully living a life of sin, the Blood of Jesus does NOT cover you anymore and, according to this Bible passage you can expect the "fearful expectation of judgment and of raging fire" - that is Hell - if you do die in your sins, "no sacrifice for sins is left, but only a fearful expectation of judgment and of raging fire that will consume the enemies of God." Hebrews 10:26-27.

If you believe the Bible at all I very much hope you believe this Scripture **as written**. God does not play around with His Word. The Lord never, ever violates His Word. If you don't believe God's clear Word, you do so at your own eternal peril. I wish there were someway to tell you these truths softly but if I do you may not understand the seriousness of what danger you are in by continuing to pursue sin. I urge you to believe the Word of God. Men may lie or be in error - but God never speaks falsely or incorrectly.

In Hebrews 10:26-31 it is referring to the person "who has trampled the Son of God underfoot, who has treated as an unholy thing the Blood of the covenant that sanctified him, and who has insulted the Spirit of grace." Most people, even though they know they are living in sin, when they read this, feel that this does not apply to them, but only to those who are blatant enemies of God such as atheists, etc. But sin is very deceptive, Hebrews 10:26-31 is referring to those WHO PROFESS CHRIST, "CONVENANT THAT SANCTIFIED HIM", but who "DELIBERATELY KEEP ON SINNING." And it states that by their deliberate sinning they are "trampling the Son of God underfoot."

I very much hope you understand the importance of what "trampling the Son of God underfoot" and "treating the Blood of the covenant as an unholy thing" really means. By your ongoing deliberate sinning you are treating the Blood of Jesus as an unholy thing and so you are despising and rejecting "the Blood of the covenant that sanctified him." You may not be doing this with words but you are doing it with actions. And actions count more than words. Recall what Jesus said in Matthew 21:28-32 about the son who said he wouldn't obey, but later did; and the son who said he would obey, but didn't. Also take note of Titus 1:16 which states that, "They claim to know God, but by their actions they deny Him."

Hence by your willful, deliberate, ongoing sinful actions you are rejecting "the Blood of the covenant that sanctified him, you," and so according to verse 26, "no sacrifice for sins is left". Please take note this means that: BY DELIBERATELY PERSISTING IN SIN, THE SACRIFICIAL BLOOD OF JESUS NO LONGER COVERS YOU. And once the Blood of Jesus no longer covers you then God will hold you personally accountable for all the sins in your life. Instead of the Blood of Jesus taking the penalty of your sins, you personally will have to pay the judgment for your sins. And as verse 27 says, the judgment for this is nothing short of eternity in Hell, "a fearful expectation of judgment and of raging fire that will consume the enemies of God."

Just like many others, at one time I thought this Hebrews 10:26-31 passage might have been talking about the disciplining of God's children but this view of simple discipline cannot be reconciled with the phrase "a fearful expectation of judgment and of raging fire that will consume the enemies of God." The penalty for those who "deliberately keep on sinning" is the same as that for the enemies of God - eternal torment in Hell. I sincerely hope that you believe God's Word as stated. We must come to understand that God never violates His Word. God ALWAYS adheres precisely to His Word - whether it is a promised blessing or a promised judgment.

Again sin is very deceptive. Some will be thinking, "But this only applies to the lost who have heard the gospel but who refuse to believe." But Hebrews 10:29 and all of Hebrews 10:26-31, also Hebrews 10:38-39, is referring to those who once believed, "the Blood of the covenant that SANCTIFIED HIM". If you have given your life to Jesus in the past, but are now willfully living a life of sin - this passage of Scripture is addressed directly to you. Not to the atheist, not to a lost person who has never known Christ, but to those who were previously SANCTIFIED. Please, please, please believe God and His Word. God never lies to us or just says things for effect. He always means precisely what He says in His Word.

A much worse and severe punishment is in store for the backslider who does not repent. I am sure you have seen or heard about believers backsliding and committing adultery and staying in that situation or those who persist in sleeping around and even living with their girlfriends or boyfriends. Or those who are consistently getting drunk and high on drugs. That my reader is deliberate and persistent sinning. And even if you don't believe it, those who do such things and don't repent and die in that state will go directly to Hell. For God never violates His Word and there is no question about it "It is a dreadful thing to fall into the hands of the living God".

Let us read a few verses that list some of the sins that will send a person to Hell. Now remember, according to Hebrews 10:26-31, those who deliberately keep on sinning forfeit the covering of the Blood of Jesus and so they will receive the full punishment for their sins in the lake of fire.

"He said to me: 'It is done. I am the Alpha and the Omega, the Beginning and the End. To him who is thirsty I will give to drink without cost from the spring of the water of life. He who overcomes will inherit all this, and I will be his God and he will be My son. But the cowardly, the unbelieving, the vile, the murderers, the sexually immoral, those who practice magic arts, the idolaters and all liars - their place will be in the fiery lake of burning sulfur. This is the second death.' " Revelations 21:6-8.

"But suppose the servant says to himself, 'My master is taking a long time in coming,' and he then begins to beat the menservants and maidservants and to eat and drink and get drunk. The master of that servant will come on a day when he does not expect him and at an hour he is not aware of. He will cut him to pieces and assign him a place with the unbelievers." Luke 12:45-46.

"Do you not know that the wicked will not inherit the kingdom of God? Do not be deceived: Neither the sexually immoral nor idolaters nor adulterers nor male prostitutes nor homosexual offenders nor thieves nor the greedy nor drunkards nor slanderers nor swindlers will inherit the kingdom of God.", 1 Corinthians 6:9-10.

Remember God is faithful and He always keeps His Word. In spite of all the Scriptures that he is aware of, the unrepentant backslider expects God to violate His Word. But the Lord cannot violate His Word. If the Lord were to violate His Word then He would be a liar. If the Lord allows you to enter Heaven in an unrepentant backslidden state then He would have to break His Word. Do you really think God is going to break His Word?

The following testimony is one that Charles G. Finney had in part of his sermons. It is about a person who was warned about his drunken lifestyle. The Lord warned this person, through a dream, that the consequence of his drunken life, if he continued in it, would result in his damnation to Hell. I realize that the inclination of so many is to doubt. But the nature of this testimony is so consistent with the warnings in the Scriptures that I believe we all should take this testimony very, very seriously. For God's Word is true and unbreakable. Yes, you can doubt God's Word. You have that choice. But the consequence is still going to be what God promises in His Word.

- Beginning of Charles Finney Excerpt -

Excerpt from the Sermon, **"The Self-Hardening Sinner's Doom".** in the book "The Way Of Salvation", Sermons by Charles G. Finney, 1891. Release by G. FREDERICK WRIGHT, OBERLIN, OHIO, September, 1891.

Sometimes he brings the lives of men into great peril, so that there shall be but a step between them and death; as if he would give this movement of his providence a voice of trumpet power to forewarn them of their coming doom. So various and striking are the ways of God's providence in which he reproves men for their sins.

God also reproves men by his Spirit. According to our Savior's teachings, the Spirit shall "reprove the world of sin, of righteousness, and of judgment." Hence when sinners are specially convicted of sin they should know that God has come in his own person to reprove them. His spirit comes to their very hearts, and makes impressions of truth and duty there revealing to the sinner his own heart, and showing him how utterly at variance it is with a heart full of divine love.

Again, I have no doubt that in the present as in former days, God reproves men of their sins by means of dreams. If all the reliable cases of this sort which have occurred since the Bible was completed were recorded, I doubt not they would fill many volumes. I am aware that some suppose this mode of divine operation upon the human mind has long ago ceased; but I think otherwise. It may have ceased to be a medium of revealing new truth doubtless it has; but it has not ceased to be employed as a means of impressing and enforcing truth already revealed.

Sometimes the great realities of the coming judgment and of the world of doom are brought out and impressed upon the mind with overwhelming force by means of dreams. When this is the case, who shall say that the hand of the Lord is not in it?

A striking instance of a dream in which the hand of the Lord may be seen, is related by President Edwards, President Edwards was a descendant of Jonathan Edwards and President of Oberlin Bible College. One of his neighbours, an intemperate, alcoholic, man, dreamed that he died and went to Hell. I will not attempt to relate here the circumstances that according to his dream occurred there. Suffice it to say that he obtained permission to return to earth on probation for one year, and was told distinctly that if he did not reform within one year, he must come back again. Upon this he awaked, undermost solemn impressions of the dreadful realities of the sinner's Hell. That very morning he went to see his pastor, Pres. Edwards, who said to him, "This is a solemn warning from God to your soul. You must give heed to it and forsake your sins, or you are a ruined man for eternity." The man made very solemn promises.

When he had retired, Edwards opened his journal and made an entry of the principal facts: the dream, the conversation, and of course the date of these events. The inebriate reformed and ran well for a time; attended church and seemed serious; but long before the year came round, he relapsed, returned to his cups, and ultimately in a fit of intoxication opened a chamber door in a shop which led down an outside stairway pitched headlong and broke his neck. Pres. Edwards turned to his journal and found that the one year from the date of his dream came round that very night, and the man's appointed time was up!

Now it is no doubt true that in general, dreams are under the control of physical law, and follow, though with much irregularity, the strain of our waking reveries; and for this reason many persons will not believe the hand of the Lord ever works in them; yet their inference is by no means legitimate; for God certainly can put his Hand upon the mind dreaming as well as upon the mind waking, and multitudes of instances in point show that He sometimes does.

Again, God reproves the sinner whenever his Spirit awakens in the mind a sense of the great danger of living in sin. I have often known sinners greatly affected with the thought of this danger the terrible danger of passing along through life in sin, exposed every hour to an eternal and remediless Hell.

Now these solemn impressions are God's kind warnings, impressed on the soul because He loves the sinner's well-being, and would fain save him if he wisely can.

Often God's Spirit gives sinners a most impressive view of the shortness of time. He makes them feel that this general truth applies in all its power to themselves that their own time is short, and that they in all probability have not long to live. I am aware that this impression sometimes originates in one's state of health; but I also know that sometimes there is good reason to recognize God's own special hand in it; and that men sometimes ascribe to nervous depression of spirits what should be ascribed directly to God himself.

Again, God often makes the impression that the present is the sinner's last opportunity to secure salvation. I know not how many such cases have fallen under my own observation, cases in which sinners have been made to feel deeply that this is to be the very last offer of mercy, and these the very last strivings of the Spirit. My observation has taught me in such cases, to expect that the result will verify the warning that this is none other than God's voice, and that God does not lie to man, but teaches most solemn and impressive truth. Oh, how does it become every sinner to listen and heed such timely warnings!

- End of Charles Finney Excerpt -

It is important to notice that the drunkard truly did repent from his sins, "The inebriate reformed and ran well for a time; attended church and seemed serious;" Later, however, he went back to his sinning and the Lord judged him and sent him to Hell - just as God had promised. As you can see God does keep His promises. He is not happy about having to judge. But God is perfectly faithful and His Word cannot be broken.

And it is very important to notice something else. This drunkard was a professing Christian, for notice the sentence, "That very morning he went to see his pastor, Pres. Edward," From this we see that the person knew very well that what he was doing was sin. Also when he repented he made an honest effort to obey Jesus. Jesus truly was his Lord during the time he ran well. But he went back to loving his sin more than Jesus and went back to his sinful drunken lifestyle. And that was his destruction. And now he is an example of God's eternal judgment.

Yes, I realize that you can come up with all sorts of possibilities that maybe Jesus never was Lord of his life, etc. But if your heart is so set on finding excuses in order to continue pursuing or justify sin in your life then you are in even greater danger than you realize.

- Hell Testimony from Dr. Roger Mills -

Excerpt from the book: "While Out Of My Body I Saw God Hell And The Living Dead" by Dr. Roger Mills

In this testimony Jesus gives Dr. Roger Mills a tour of Hell and shows him many people in torment there. In this testimony Jesus is explaining that the backslidden will be sent to Hell.

- Beginning of Testimony by Dr. Roger Mills -

While standing in front of that silver door, I noticed hanging above the entrance of the door was a written inscription. God noticed me looking at the written inscription. He said to me, "The writing you are looking at is Greek writing. It reads: *The Door That Leads to Outer Darkness.* In this place called Outer Darkness, I will reveal to you the biggest secret that Satan doesn't want anyone on Earth to know about. The secret is that there are severe punishments awaiting the willfully ignorant person that practices sin. The punishments also await those who do not want to have anything to do with your Lord and Savior, Jesus Christ or my Holy Book, which you call the Bible. Look, listen and learn. Severe punishments await all of whom I have called to serve Me, who then become backslidden, especially preachers who have become hypocritical and backslidden, and for all the disobedient children of God that will not stop practicing sin since they have come into the knowledge of the truth of My Holy Word, which you call the Holy Bible."

"No man, having put his hand to the plough, and looking back, is fit for the Kingdom of God." Luke 9:62 KJV.

Just then, I asked God this question: "What type of sins do people practice that will cause them to come here to the Outer Darkness of Hell?" God looked at me and immediately He answered and said, "The biggest sin is this: to reject the Savior, Jesus Christ. It is not what a person does that makes them a sinner; it is what they haven't done. That is to accept Jesus Christ as their Lord and personal Savior, who died on the cross for everyone that ever lived throughout the entire world."

God continued to say, "If anyone breaks the Ten Commandments willfully, and will not stop to confess and repent of their sins, at the time of their death they will come to this place of Hell in Outer Darkness. I want you to look, listen and learn. Those who practice telling lies, stealing, homosexuality, adultery, fornication, idolatry, murder of any kind - such as abortion - theft, disobedience to parents, child abuse and child pornography, those who illegally buy drugs and illegally sell drugs, and those who illegally use drugs for pleasure, whosoever practices such things and are not willing to repent, they shall have their part in Gehenna - the Lake of Fire with Satan and those who blaspheme the Holy Ghost. Roger, soon I will let you see and meet persons who are here in the Outer Darkness of Hell, who have practiced all of these great sins."

Then God looked at me with tears in His eyes, and He said to me, "Roger, please let this be known. I do not send anyone to Hell. They send themselves when they refuse to practice all that is written in My Holy Book. Severe punishments await the backslidden preachers such as apostles, prophets, evangelists, pastors, teachers, priests, and bishops, of whom I will allow you to see later during our tour of the Outer Darkness of Hell. My son, I want you to understand that satan hates preachers who I have called to preach the Gospel of my Holy Word ! Remember, what I said in my Holy Word, in the gospel of Matthew, the 25th chapter and verse 30."

"cast ye the unprofitable servant into Outer Darkness: there shall be weeping and gnashing of teeth." - Matthew 25:30 KJV.

--- End of Dr. Roger Mills Testimony ---

CHAPTER 6

TORMENTS IN HELL FOR BACKSLIDERS ARE WORSE THAN FOR UNBELIEVERS

As you know all unbelievers will be condemned to Hell at their death. This we know from many Scriptures. For example Jesus Himself said so in Revelations 21:8, "But the cowardly, THE UNBELIEVING, the vile, the murderers, the sexually immoral, those who practice magic arts, the idolaters and all liars - their place will be in the fiery lake of burning sulfur. This is the second death. "

For the unbeliever, Hell is a place of relentless and excruciating pain and torment. And everybody in Hell longs for even the slightest reduction in the torment. For notice what the rich man said in Luke 16:23-24, "And being in torment in Hades, he lifted up his eyes and saw Abraham afar off, and Lazarus in his bosom. Then he cried and said, 'Father Abraham, have mercy on me, and send Lazarus that he may dip the tip of his finger in water and cool my tongue; for I am tormented in this flame.' "

The rich man wasn't even asking for a stop to his eternal punishment in Hell - he knew he fully deserved it and that it would never stop. He was just hoping for even the slightest reduction in its fiery torment, "that he may dip the tip of his finger in water and cool my tongue; for I am tormented in this flame."

The sinner in Hell will wish that he had committed one less sin. Because then the fire would be that much less intense. He will even wish that he had never been born or that his life on earth had been shortened by decades, even one less year, one less month, one less week, even one less day - because he would have sinned that much less. Any reduction in torment is longed for by those in Hell. It is ironic, but the sinner while on earth wishes for more time to "live it up" in sin. But in Hell he will wish that his life had been drastically shortened. It boggles the human mind but this is the reality of Hell. It is not comfortable to think about it, but it is nonetheless true.

An illustration of how terrible Hell truly is, can be seen from the following testimony taken from the book, <u>A Divine Revelation Of Hell</u>, by Mary K. Baxter, Whitaker House, 1993. In this book the author describes what Jesus showed her about Hell. In fact Jesus took Mary into the spirit realm and into actual Hell and showed her several people who are condemned there. This was done over a course of 40 days. Mary Baxter saw the torment and suffering that the damned were and are suffering. I have read this book several times and have compared what is described in Baxter's book with the Bible. I also have prayed and listened to the Holy Spirit concerning the author's truthfulness.

I believe what the author is saying because: 1. It is very consistent with all that the Bible has to say about Hell, and, 2. The Holy Spirit has confirmed in my heart that what the author says is a true testimony. Also take note of the scripture passage 2 Corinthians 12:1-4 where the Apostle Paul states: "It is not expedient for me doubtless to glory. I will come to visions and revelations of the Lord. I knew a man in Christ above fourteen years ago, whether in the body, I cannot tell; or whether out of the body, I cannot tell; God knoweth;, such an one caught up to the third heaven. And I knew such a man, whether in the body, or out of the body, I cannot tell; God knoweth;, How that he was caught up into paradise, and heard unspeakable words, which it is not lawful for a man to utter.", 1 Corinthians 12:1-4.

From this passage we can conclude that believers having spiritual revelations of the after life, either Heaven or Hell, is not impossible and has happened before, in accordance with what God wills. Considering that God is Sovereign and all powerful and has created everything - the heavens, the earth, the plants, the animals, man, everything - surely it is not impossible for God to give an individual a spiritual revelation. For any of us humans to try to put restrictions on what God can or cannot do is not our place. We can't anyway.

Again God is Sovereign. Everything that God does, He does with wisdom and with purpose. Our place is to believe Him and obey Him. What Paul said in 1 Corinthians 12:1-14 shows that God can and does give spiritual revelations to those He wills. It is as Charles G. Finney stated, "I am aware that some suppose this mode of divine operation upon the human mind has long ago ceased; but I think otherwise. It may have ceased to be a medium of revealing new truth doubtless it has; but it has not ceased to be employed as a means of impressing and enforcing truth already revealed." God uses the types of divine revelations that He gave Mary K. Baxter to reinforce those things He has already stated in His Word.

Anyway, the book begins with Jesus appearing to Mary K. Baxter. Jesus then takes Mary into the spirit realm and into Hell.

Beginning of Excerpt From, A Divine Revelation Of Hell, by Mary K. Baxter.

Jesus takes Mary K. Baxter into Hell and tells her:, "These things you are about to see will always be with you. The world must know about the reality of Hell. Many sinners and even some of My people do not believe that Hell is real. You have been chosen by Me to reveal these truths to them. Everything I will show you about Hell and all the other things I will show you are true."

…Jesus and I stepped from the tunnel onto a path with wide swaths of land on each side of it. There were pits of fire everywhere as far as the eye could see. The pits were four feet across and three feet deep and shaped like a bowl. Jesus said, "There are many pits like this in the left leg of Hell. Come, I will show you some of them."

I stood beside Jesus on the path and looked into one of the pits. Brimstone was embedded in the side of the pit and glowed red like hot coals of fire. In the center of the pit was a lost soul who had died and gone to Hell. Fire began at the bottom of the pit, swept upward and clothed the lost soul in flames. In a moment the fire would die down to embers, then with a rushing sound would sweep back over the tormented soul in the pit.

I looked and saw that the lost soul in the pit was caged inside a skeleton form. "My Lord," I cried at the sight, "Can't you let them out?" How awful was the sight! I thought, This could be me. I said, "Lord, how sad it is to see and know that a living soul is in there."

I heard a cry from the center of the first pit. I saw a soul in the form of a skeleton, crying, "Jesus, have mercy!"

"Oh, Lord!" I said. It was the voice of a woman. I looked at her and wanted to pull her out of the fire. The sight of her broke my heart. The skeleton form of a woman with a dirty-grey mist inside was talking to Jesus. In shock, I listened to her. Decayed flesh hung by shreds from her bones, and, as it burned, it fell off into the bottom of the pit. Where her eyes had once been were now only empty sockets. She had no hair.

The fire started at her feet in small flames and grew as it climbed up and over her body. The woman seemed to be constantly burning, even when the flames were only embers. From deep down inside her came cries and groans of despair, "Lord, Lord, I want out of here!"

She kept reaching out to Jesus. I looked at Jesus, and there was great sorrow on His face. Jesus said to me, "My child, you are here with Me to let the world know that sin results in death, that Hell is real."

I looked at the woman again, and worms were crawling out of the bones of her skeleton. They were not harmed by the fire. Jesus said, "She knows and feels those worms inside."

"God, have mercy!" I cried as the fire reached its peak and the horrible burning started all over again. Great cries and deep sobs shook the form of this woman-soul. She was lost. There was no way out. "Jesus, why is she here?" I said in a small voice, for I was very scared.

Jesus said, "Come."

The path we were on was a circuitous one, twisting in and out between these pits of fire as far as I could see. The cries of the living dead, mixed with moans and hideous screams, came to my ears from all directions. There were no quiet times in Hell. The smell of dead and decaying flesh hung thickly in the air.

We came to the next pit. Inside this pit, which was the same size as the other one, was another skeleton form. A man's voice cried from the pit, saying, Lord, have mercy on me!" Only when they spoke could I tell whether the soul was a man or woman.

Great wailing sobs came from this man. "I'm so sorry, Jesus. Forgive me. Take me out of here. I have been in this place of torment for years. I beg You, let me out!" Great sobs shook his skeletal frame as he begged, "Please, Jesus, let me out!" I looked at Jesus and saw that He too was crying.

"Lord Jesus," the man cried out from the burning pit, "haven't I suffered enough for my sins? It has been forty years since my death."

Jesus said, "It is written, 'The just shall live by faith!' All mockers and unbelievers shall have their part in the lake of fire. You would not believe the truth. Many times My people were sent to you to show you the way, but you would not listen to them. You laughed at them and refused the gospel. Even though I died on a cross for you, you mocked Me and would not repent of your sins. My Father gave you many opportunities to be saved. If only you had listened!" Jesus wept.

"I know, Lord, I know!" the man cried. "But I repent now."

"It is too late," said Jesus. "Judgment is set."

The man continued, "Lord, some of my people are coming here, for they also will not repent. Please, Lord, let me go tell them that they must repent of their sins while they are still on earth. I do not want them to come here."

Jesus said, "They have preachers, teachers, elders - all ministering the gospel. They will tell them. They also have the advantages of the modern communications systems and many other ways to learn of Me. I sent workers to them that they might believe and be saved. If they will not believe when they hear the gospel, neither will they be persuaded though one rises from the dead."

At this, the man became very angry and began to curse. Evil, blasphemous words came from him. I looked on in horror as the flames rose up and his dead, decaying flesh began to burn and fall off. Inside this dead shell of a man, I saw his soul. It looked like a dirty-gray mist, and it filled the inside of his skeleton.

I turned to Jesus and cried, "Lord, how horrible!"

Jesus said, "Hell is real; the judgment is real. I love them so, My child. This is only the beginning of the frightful things I have to show you. There is much more to come. Tell the world for Me that Hell is real, that men and women must repent of their sins. Come, follow Me. We must go on."

...From the pit a woman's voice spoke to Jesus. She stood in the center of the flames, and they covered her whole body. Her bones were full of worms and dead flesh. As the flames flickered up around her, she raised her hands towards Jesus, crying, "Let me out of here. I will give You my heart now, Jesus. I will tell others about Your forgiveness. I will witness for You. I beg You, please let me out!"

Jesus said, "My Word is true, and it declares that all must repent and turn from their sins and ask Me to come into their lives if they are to escape this place. Through My blood there is forgiveness of sins. I am faithful and just and will forgive all those who come to Me. I will not cast them out."

He turned, looked at the woman and said, "If you had listened to Me and had come to Me and repented, I would have forgiven you."

The woman asked, "Lord, is there no way out of here?"

Jesus spoke very softly. "Woman," He said, "you were given many opportunities to repent, but you hardened your heart and would not. And you knew My Word said that all whoremongers will have their part in the lake of fire."

Jesus turned to me and said, "This woman had sinful affairs with many men, and she caused many homes to be broken apart. Yet through all this, I loved her still. I came to her not in condemnation but with salvation. I sent many of My servants to her that she might repent of her evil ways, but she would not. When she was a young woman, I called her, but she continued to do evil. She did many wrongs, yet I would have forgiven her if she had come to Me. Satan entered into her, and she grew bitter and would not forgive others.

"She went to church just to get men. She found them and seduced them. If she had only come to Me, her sins would all have been washed away by My blood. Part of her wanted to serve Me, but you cannot serve God and satan at the same time. Every person must make a choice as to whom they will serve.

...Jesus and I walked on 'through the pits. I wanted to pull each person I passed from the fire and rush them to the feet of Jesus. I wept much.

In the next pit was a woman on her knees, as if looking for something. Her skeletal form also was full of holes. Her bones were showing through, and her torn dress was on fire. Her head was bald, and there were only holes where her eyes and nose were supposed to be. A small fire was burning around her feet where she was kneeling, and she clawed the sides of the brimstone pit. The fire clung to her hands, and dead flesh kept falling off as she dug.

Tremendous sobs shook her. "Oh Lord, Oh Lord," she cried, "I want out." As we watched, she finally got to the top of the pit with her feet. I thought she was going to get out when a large demon with great wings that seemed to be broken at the top and hung down his sides ran to her. His color was brownish-black, and he had hair all over his large form. His eyes were set far back into his head, and he was about the size of a large grizzly bear. The demon rushed up to the woman and pushed her very hard backward into the pit and fire. I watched in horror as she fell. I felt so sorry for her. I wanted to take her into my arms and hold her, to ask God to heal her and take her out of there.

Jesus knew my thoughts and said, "My child, judgment has been set. God has spoken. Even when she was a child, I called and called her to repent and to serve Me. When she was sixteen years old, I came to her and said, 'I love you. Give your life to Me, and come follow Me, for I have called you for a special purpose.' I called all her life, but she would not listen. She said, "Someday I will serve You. I have no time for You now. No time, no time, I have my life of fun. No time, no time to serve You, Jesus. Tomorrow I will.' Tomorrow never came, for she waited too long."

The woman cried out to Jesus, "My soul is truly in torment. There is no way out. I know that I wanted the world instead of You, Lord. I wanted riches, fame and fortune, and I got it. I could buy anything I wanted; I was my own boss. I was the prettiest, best-dressed woman of my time. And I had riches, fame and fortune, but I found I could not take them with me in death. Oh Lord, Hell is horrible. I have no rest day or night. I am always in pain and torment. Help me, Lord," she cried.

The woman looked up at Jesus so longingly and said, "My sweet Lord, if only I had listened to you! I will regret that forever. I planned to serve You someday - when I got ready. I thought You would always be there for me. But how wrong I was! I was one of the most sought-after women of my time for my beauty. I knew God was calling me to repent. All my life He drew me with cords of love, and I thought I could use God like I used everyone else. He would always be there. Oh yes, I used God! He would try so hard to get me to serve Him, while all the time I thought I didn't need Him. Oh, how wrong I was! For satan began to use me, and I began to serve satan more and more. At the last I loved him more than God. I loved to sin and would not turn to God.

"Satan used my beauty and my money, and all my thoughts turned to how much power he would give me. Even then, God continued to draw me. But I thought, I have tomorrow or the next day. Then one day while riding in a car, my driver ran into a house, and I was killed. Lord, please let me out." As she spoke her bony hands and arms reached out to Jesus while the flames continued to burn her.

Jesus said, "The judgment is set."

Tears fell down His cheeks as we moved to the next pit. I was crying inside about the horrors of Hell. "Dear Lord," I cried, "the torment is too real. When a soul comes here, there is no hope, no life, no love. Hell is too real." No way out, I thought. She must burn forever in these flames.

"Time is running out," Jesus said. "We will come back tomorrow."

Friend, if you are living in sin, please repent. If you have been born again and have turned your back on God, repent and turn back to Him now. Live good and stand for truth. Wake up before it is too late, and you can spend forever with the Lord in Heaven.

Jesus spoke again, "Hell has a body, like a human form, lying on her back in the center of the earth. Hell is shaped like a human body - very large and with many chambers of torment. "Remember to tell the people of earth that Hell is real. Millions of lost souls are here, and more are coming every day. On the Great Judgment Day death and Hell will be cast into the lake of fire; that will be the second death."

End Of Revelation of Hell Excerpt.

As mentioned previously, after reading Baxter's book several times, comparing what is being said to the Bible, and listening to the Holy Spirit, I very much believe that this testimony is truthful. I suggest that you compare what is being said with what is written in the Bible. You cannot be led astray if you read and compare testimony or what is being said to see if it is supported by the Bible. For this reason I present some scriptures that are relevant:

"But the cowardly, the unbelieving, the vile, the murderers, the sexually immoral, those who practice magic arts, the idolaters and all liars - their place will be in the fiery lake of burning sulfur. This is the second death." Revelation 21:8.

"Do you not know that the wicked will not inherit the kingdom of God? Do not be deceived: Neither the sexually immoral nor idolaters nor adulterers nor male prostitutes nor homosexual offenders nor thieves nor the greedy nor drunkards nor slanderers nor swindlers will inherit the kingdom of God." 1 Corinthians 6:9-10.

"For if God did not spare angels when they sinned, but sent them to Hell, putting them into gloomy dungeons to be held for judgment; if He did not spare the ancient world when He brought the flood on its ungodly people, but protected Noah, a preacher of righteousness, and seven others; if He condemned the cities of Sodom and Gomorrah by burning them to ashes, and made them an example of what is going to happen to the ungodly; . if this is so, then the Lord knows how to . hold the unrighteous for the day of judgment, while continuing their punishment.", 2 Peter 2:4-9.

"If your hand causes you to sin, cut it off. It is better for you to enter life maimed than with two hands to go into Hell, where the fire never goes out. And if your foot causes you to sin, cut it off. It is better for you to enter life crippled than to have two feet and be thrown into Hell. And if your eye causes you to sin, pluck it out. It is better for you to enter the kingdom of God with one eye than to have two eyes and be thrown into Hell, where "'their worm does not die, and the fire is not quenched.' " Mark 9:43-48.

"Whoever believes in the Son has eternal life, but whoever rejects the Son will not see life, for God's wrath remains on him.", John 3:36.

As you can see from the above testimony, the punishment in Hell for non-believers is intensely painful and never ending. As bad as the punishment is for the non-believers it is even worse for backsliders - those who once came to Jesus but went back into the mire of sin, those who deliberately keep on sinning. When God gives us warnings and examples of His judgment either in the Word or in revelations, or in actual experiences He does not exaggerate. God means precisely what He says in His unbreakable Word.

Even if you are not sure that the above testimony is true, God's Word still remains true as Revelations 21:8, 1 Corinthians 6:9-10, 2 Peter 2:4-9, Mark 9:43-48, John 3:36 and many other Scriptures state. However, bad you think Hell is - in reality it is much worse. Just like we don't comprehend how infinite God is in His blessings toward His true children, we don't comprehend how infinite God's wrath is towards the wicked. As Psalm 90:11 states, "Who knows the power of Your anger? For Your wrath is as great as the fear that is due You." Notice that God's wrath is as great as the fear that is DUE Him - and not the fear that people actually express toward Him. Those who deliberately sin so casually don't fear God. But if they realized what was truly in store for them because of those sins they would not be acting so rebelliously. In the midst of this you must also understand that God takes absolutely no pleasure in destroying the wicked. As the Lord says in Ezekiel 33:11, "'As surely as I live,' declares the Sovereign LORD, 'I take no pleasure in the death of the wicked, but rather that they turn from their ways and live. Turn! Turn from your evil ways!' "

Again I realize all this sounds so fearful but the reality is that the true terror of Hell, being depicted here in words, does not even come close to the real terror of the real Hell. I know I am repeating myself, but God really did mean His first warning to us - all of mankind - when He told us, "When you eat of it, evil, you will surely DIE." Genesis 2:17.

I mentioned the following before, but I think it bears repeating: How could it be a just thing that God would send a lost sinner, who never knew Christ, to Hell for eternity for his sins, and not send someone who came to know Jesus but went back to sinning in the same detestable way as the lost sinner? Do you really think God has a double standard? That sinning is not acceptable for the non-believer, but it is allowable for God's people? That those who are supposed to be righteous can get away with a sinful lifestyle, but that the non-believer cannot? Is this not calling evil good, and good evil? Is this not calling bitter sweet, and sweet bitter?

If you believe that God will side with you in unrepentant deliberate persistent sinning you are tragically, tragically mistaken. It is not that God doesn't love you. He loves you dearly and desires greatly for you to return to Him. But if you are caught dead in unrepentant deliberate persistent detestable sinning, whether it be immorality, or drunkenness, or drugs or witchcraft, etc. Revelations 21:8, 1 Corinthians 6:9-10, you will end up directly in Hell. Again I realize these are strong words, but considering just the scriptures presented in this book how can we conclude otherwise?

Now regarding the fate of unrepentant backsliders - both those who profess to know Christ and those who actually came to Him in the past, but who now deliberately keep on sinning - let us read what Jesus said in Luke 12:45-48. And keep in mind that in this passage, Jesus is addressing His servants - those who profess to believe and serve Him: "But suppose the servant says to himself, `My master is taking a long time in coming,' and he then begins to beat the menservants and maidservants and to eat and drink and get drunk. The master of that servant will come on a day when he does not expect him and at an hour he is not aware of. He will cut him to pieces and assign him A PLACE WITH THE UNBELIEVERS, HELL. That servant who knows his master's will and does not get ready or does not do what his master wants will be beaten with many blows. But the one who does not know and does things deserving punishment will be beaten with few blows. From everyone who has been given much, much will be demanded; and from the one who has been entrusted with much, much more will be asked." Luke 12:45-48.

With this in mind, 2 Peter 2:20-21 reveals that the torment promised for those who previously knew Christ, but who went back to a sinful lifestyle, is **much worse** than for the unbeliever who never knew Christ. The backslider, he who deliberately keeps on sinning, knows extremely well that the sin he is involved in, deserves eternal punishment in Hell - much more so than what the unbeliever knows it. However, the unrepentant professing Christian has been deceived into believing that even in an unrepentant state all his sins are still under the Blood of Jesus. But Hebrews 10:26-31, Luke 12:45-48, and now 2 Peter 2:20-21 says the exact opposite.

Because the unrepentant backslider knows extremely well the just consequence for his sin, the torment for him in Hell will be that much more extreme. However painful the torment will be for the non-believer, the pain for the backslider - those believers who went back to a life of sin - will be even more intense. And remember, any reduction in the torment is greatly desired by everyone in Hell. If you read and **believe** Hebrews 10:26-31, Luke 12:45-48, and 2 Peter 2:20-21, and other Scriptures that warn about falling away, there is **no other** biblically consistent conclusion that can be reached.

Again just like the Hebrews 10:26-31 passage, the passage in 2 Peter 2:20-21 is not difficult to understand. It is very advisable to read it and re-read it, and read it again, as many times as is necessary to believe this Scripture - AS WRITTEN! Yes, you can turn to the "Once Saved Always Saved" teachers to try to "explain away" this Scripture - but the fires in Hell, for those who sin in this way, are not going to diminish in their intensity.

It is wise counsel for anyone, who is currently living in a sinful lifestyle, to fear God intensely **now** - before risking one more day - and let that fear of God guide you to utterly reject sin totally from your life. In fact, pray earnestly for God to impart the fear of God into your heart so that you can turn away from sin and into the Father's loving hands. There is no one who loves you more than God the Father - your loving Creator. The sacrifice of His One and Only begotten Son proves how much He loves you. He never intended for Hell to be your fate. But God is also perfectly just and perfectly holy and He cannot allow any unrepentant, sinful, unclean person into His Kingdom - even those who previously repented but then went back to a life of sin.

Let us now read 2 Peter 2:20-21 with a true intent to believe and with the fear of God in our heart:

2 Peter 2:20-21 "If they have escaped the corruption of the world by knowing our Lord and Savior Jesus Christ and are again entangled in it and overcome, they are worse off at the end than they were at the beginning. It would have been better for them not to have known the way of righteousness, than to have known it and then to turn their backs on the sacred command that was passed on to them." NIV.

Here the Apostle Peter is talking about those who at one time repented, "escaped the corruption of the world", and came to "know our Lord and Savior Jesus Christ." However, later these same people were again "entangled" in "the corruption of the world" by sinning and disobeying Jesus. Notice that at one time they had "known the way of righteousness", verse 21, just like everyone who has given their lives to Jesus. But now they were back into doing the corrupt things of the world - sinning and disregarding the commandments of the Lord.

And what was the sacred command? The sacred command was truly receiving and remaining in Jesus as Lord of their lives - by obeying Jesus and always staying away from sin in their lives. At one time, they truly repented, renounced and rejected all pursuit of sin and committed to follow and obey Jesus. But now they willfully chose to go back to pursuing sin. They, of course, remember the previous commitment that they had made to Jesus. But now, in order to pursue the pleasures of sin, they broke the covenant of obedience that they previously had with Jesus. Because of this 2 Peter 2:20 states that they are now "worse off at the end than they were at the beginning."

Again, I wish there was some softer way to submit the words on these pages to you, but the danger you are in and the seriousness of this matter requires that I be as direct and truthful as I can be. Please believe God and His Word.

At the beginning, before you knew Jesus as Lord, you were on the path to Hell - as are all lost and non-believing sinners. But now, . now, according to 2 Peter 2:20-21, you are even worse off than you were as a lost sinner before you knew Christ. After having known Christ, the guilt of your sinful life is now much worse than before knowing Christ. For now you know the penalty that a sinful life deserves but because of your love of your sin you are back to pursuing sin instead of pursuing Jesus Christ. In other words Jesus is not Lord of your life anymore. Jesus even warned us in Matthew 7:21 that, "Not everyone who says to Me, 'Lord, Lord,' shall enter the kingdom of Heaven, but he who does the will of My Father in Heaven."

Some of you readers are thinking. "But my sin is not that bad. God will not send me to Hell." The question you need to ask yourself is: "Am I entangled again in deliberately sinning?" Please answer the question honestly. Call a spade a spade. Kidding yourself is not going to change the facts. In fact, kidding yourself is deadly.

If you find yourself resisting even answering this question, shouldn't that be a sign to you that you are trying to avoid being honest with yourself and with God? If this is your case, I would be extremely fearful of what God's judgment is going to be at the minute of my death. Many say that we should avoid fear. This is correct when the fear is with respect to anything or anyone other than God, but the Word of God actually **commands** that we fear God. "Fear God and give Him glory, because the hour of His judgment has come.",Revelations 14:7a. For "the fear of the Lord makes men turn from evil." Proverbs 16:6, and "the fear of the Lord is the beginning of wisdom, and they who live by it grow in understanding." Psalm 111:10.

So with the fear of the Lord in your heart please answer this question honestly and humbly: Are you entangled again in deliberate sinning?

If the answer is yes, then 2 Peter 2:20-21 and Hebrews 10:26-31 applies to you. Again not to the atheist, not to the lost sinner who has never known Christ, but to you - you who "once have known the way of righteousness" in Christ. Don't you know how deadly and deceptive sin is? It destroys your sight on how ugly and wicked your sin really is. That is why it is absolutely essential that you believe God's Word about your condition.

The Lord does not give you idle words in Hebrews 10:26-31 and 2 Peter 2:20-21, He KNOWS and tells you precisely your condition and where it is leading you. God desires - even yearns to forgive and cleanse you, and cover you again with the precious Blood of Jesus. But if you persist in your unrepentant state, He cannot. He has given His Word and Holy Standard in Hebrews 10:26-31 and 2 Peter 2:20-21 as well as many other Scriptures.

It is like a sickness where you might feel ok, no major problems felt, but you go to the doctor and he tells you, you have the beginning of cancer and you need treatment immediately. Because you feel ok, you may choose not to believe the doctor and so you tell Him or yourself. No, I'm ok. I feel fine. Yes, you may feel fine now, but unless you get treatment, in 10 months you will be very dead! The doctor KNOWS what he is talking about. If you want to live you will trust the doctor's Word and you will get treatment immediately! This is exactly the urgency that you need to have with the Word of God about your sinful condition. In fact you should have a much greater urgency, since we are talking about your eternal life and not about physical life.

What is stated in 2 Peter 2:20-21 is the same as what is stated in Ezekiel 33:12-13 - where it states that prior righteousness, when you truly followed Jesus and obeyed Him, will not be remembered if you go back to doing evil and sinful actions. Listen to **and believe** what the Lord **promises** in Ezekiel 33:12-13.

"The righteousness of the righteous man will not save him when he disobeys, and the wickedness of the wicked man will not cause him to fall when he turns from it. The righteous man, if he sins, will not be allowed to live because of his former righteousness.' If I tell the righteous man that he will surely live, but then he trusts in his righteousness and does evil, none of the righteous things he has done will be remembered; HE WILL DIE FOR THE EVIL HE HAS DONE." Ezekiel 33:12-13.

Doing the will of the Father is living a holy, godly life by obeying Him. Even though by your words you may be professing Jesus as Lord, the disobedient sinful actions of your life, and heart, that you are persisting in, are denying that Lordship. You may be able to fool fallible man or even deceive yourself, but there is no fooling God. He knows very well the true motives and intentions of your heart. God has given you every ability to obey Him. Every commandment that God gives you He also gives you the power to fulfill. And He will supply all the power you need to overcome - if you really truly desire to put away sin and follow Him.

But if you still insist on disobeying Him, by continuing in your sin - you do have that freedom of will - but your choice of living a disobedient sinful life carries an eternal price. And according to 2 Peter 2:20-21 that price is a greater suffering in Hell, "they are worse off at the end than they were at the beginning". There are degrees of torment in Hell - and it is in direct proportion to the light you have. And obviously those who remained in a lost state never having known Jesus had far less light than those who did receive Jesus as their Lord, but who later went back to a sinful lifestyle. That is why Peter was inspired to say what he did in 2 Peter 2:20-21.

I know some of you may feel that I am judging you, but this is really a heartfelt warning. Because I love you. I cannot bear to see anyone go to Hell. I urge you sincerely and with much tears, please believe God's Word as written. Repent from pursuing sin. Pay any price to get out of your sin.

If you are living in sin with another person, or causing them to sin with you, you must realize that you are contributing to their sin and to their damnation also. So not only are you damning yourself, you are also dragging someone else to Hell with you. And please notice that if you continue in deliberate sinning Hebrews 10:26-31, 2 Peter 2:20-21, and Luke 12:45-46 are all promising Hell. Again, this is not something I made up. It is God's precious and truthful Word. Even though the other person may not understand it, the most loving thing you can do for that other person, that you are living in sin with, is to separate completely from them and hence stop causing them to participate in the sin with you. It is painful and not comfortable - but eternity in Hell, for both of you, is much more painful and is eternal. There is not even any comparison.

True repentance is not merely a sentimental feeling or merely a confession of your sin without any change of action. To repent means to completely turn around from pursuing sin toward now pursuing full and complete obedience to Jesus. Repentance is an act of the will. Don't wait until you feel like repenting because chances are you won't feel like repenting until you are in the torments of Hell. Repentance is an act of the will and is a solemn, deliberate decision to obey Jesus completely no matter what the cost - and it is followed up with real actions. Not just words but actions!, Recall what Jesus said in Matthew 21:28-32 about the son who said he would obey but didn't, or what John the Baptist said: "produce fruit in keeping with repentance." Luke 3:8.

There is absolutely no way that you can both serve Jesus and sin. If you deliberately keep on sinning your lord, the one you follow and belong to, is satan and not Jesus. The devil's servants serve him by sinning, and Jesus' servants serve Him by obeying and NOT sinning. And please realize that this last statement, also, is not something I made up, for read and hear what 1 John 3:7-8 is saying:

"Dear children, do not let anyone lead you astray. He who does what is right is righteous, just as He is righteous. HE WHO DOES WHAT IS SINFUL IS OF THE DEVIL, because the devil has been sinning from the very beginning." 1 John 3:7-8.

I hope you understand that this warning is meant to awake and help you. It is better to get a warning before you die rather than no warning at all and end up in Hell forever. Don't you see the compassion and grace that Jesus is extending to you right now by bringing you this word. Some people may never get the warning that you have been provided here. Please recognize the offer of grace that Jesus is extending to you again. You received it once in the past. Why not receive His grace again? Do you love your sin that much - that you would deny Christ by your actions and risk eternity in Hell forever? I hope this is not your heart. Please let this not be your heart.

As an illustration of how horrible judgment is going to be for those who deliberately keep on sinning, I present another part of the divine revelation of Hell that the Lord gave to Mary K. Baxter. From this we see a fearful example of God judging not only unbelievers but also those who once knew Him but who turned their backs on Jesus and are back living a life of sin.

Beginning of Excerpt, From "Divine Revelation Of Hell", by Mary K. Baxter.

As we walked on through Hell, Jesus and I came upon a very large and very dark man. He was enshrouded in darkness and had the appearance of an angel. He was holding something in his left hand.

Jesus said, "This place is called outer darkness."

I heard weeping and gnashing of teeth. No where before had there been such utter hopelessness as I felt in this place. The angel that stood before us had no wings. He looked to be about thirty feet tall, and he knew exactly what he was doing. He had a large disk in his left hand and was turning slowly with this disk lifted up high as though he was getting ready to throw it. There was a fire in the middle of the disk, and blackness on the outer edge. The angel held his hand beneath the disk and reached far back in order to get more leverage. I wondered who this giant angel was and what he was about to do.

Jesus knew my thoughts and said again, "This is outer darkness. Remember that my Word says, 'The children of the kingdom shall be cast out into outer darkness: there shall be weeping and gnashing of teeth.' "

"Lord," I said, "You mean your servants are here?"

"Yes," said Jesus, "servants that turned back after I called them. Servants who loved the world more than Me and went back to wallowing in the mire of sin. Servants that would not stand for the truth and for holiness. It is better that one never starts than to turn back after beginning to serve Me."

"Believe Me," Jesus said, "if you sin, you have an advocate with the Father. If you repent of your sins, I will be faithful to cleanse you of all unrighteousness. But if you will not repent, I will come in a time you think not, and you will be cut off with the unbelievers and cast into outer darkness."

I watched the dark angel as he cast the large disk far, far out into the darkness.

"My Word means just what it says: they 'shall be cast into outer darkness.'"

And then, immediately, Jesus and I were in the air following this disk through space. We came to the outside of the disk and stood looking in.

There was a fire in the center of the disk, and people were swimming in and out, over and under the flaming waves. There were no demons or evil spirits here, only souls burning in a sea of fire.

Outside the disk was the blackest of darkness. Only the light from the flames in the disk illuminated the night air. In that light I saw people trying to swim to the edges of the disk. Some of them would almost reach the sides when a suction force from inside the disk would drag them back into the flames. I watched as their forms turned to skeletons with misty-gray souls. I knew then that this was just another part of Hell.

And then I saw, as in a vision, angels opening seals. Nations and kingdoms appeared to be locked beneath them. As the angels broke the seals, men and women, boys and girls marched straight into the flames.

I watched in ghastly fascination, wondering if I knew any of the fallen servants of the Lord who were marching past. I could not turn my head away from the sight of souls marching into the fire, and no one was trying to stop them.

I cried, "Lord, please stop them before they reach the fire!"

But Jesus said, "He who has ears should hear. He who has eyes should see. My child, cry out against sin and evil. Tell my servants to be faithful and to call upon the name of the Lord. I am taking you through this awful place so that you can tell them about Hell."

Jesus continued, "Some will not believe you. Some will say God is too good to send men and women to Hell. But tell them My Word is true. Tell them that the fearful and unbelieving will have their part in the lake of fire."

End of Excerpt by Mary K. Baxter.

Relevant Scriptures:

"But the children of the kingdom shall be cast out into outer darkness: there shall be weeping and gnashing of teeth.", Matthew 8:12, KJV.

"Therefore keep watch, because you do not know on what day your Lord will come. But understand this: If the owner of the house had known at what time of night the thief was coming, he would have kept watch and would not have let his house be broken into. So you also must be ready, because the Son of Man will come at an hour when you do not expect him.

But suppose that servant is wicked and says to himself, `My master is staying away a long time,' and he then begins to beat his fellow servants and to eat and drink with drunkards. The master of that servant will come on a day when he does not expect him and at an hour he is not aware of. He will cut him to pieces and assign him a place with the hypocrites, where there will be weeping and gnashing of teeth." Matthew 24:42-44,48-51.

In the above testimony by Mary K. Baxter, notice how precisely Jesus stated what He inspired Peter to write in 2 Peter 2:20-22.

"If they have escaped the corruption of the world by knowing our Lord and Savior Jesus Christ and are again entangled in it and overcome, they are worse off at the end than they were at the beginning. It would have been better for them not to have known the way of righteousness, than to have known it and then to turn their backs on the sacred command that was passed on to them. Of them the proverbs are true: 'A dog returns to its vomit,' and, 'A sow that is washed goes back to her wallowing in the mud.' ", 2 Peter 2:20-22, NIV.

As you can see from the above scriptures and testimony, judgment is not confined only to non-believers who refused to come to Jesus for salvation. God also will condemn those who once knew and obeyed Him but are now disobeying and living a life of sin. The condemnation is especially severe for these people.

If you are one of these people take heed to what the Spirit is telling you. If this is your case, Jesus brought you to salvation once but if you are living in sin and are disobeying God, pay careful attention to what 2 Thessalonians 1:8,9 is saying: "and <u>those who do not obey the gospel</u> of our Lord Jesus Christ. These shall be punished with everlasting destruction, Hell, from the presence of the Lord and from the glory of His power." . Also take heed of Hebrews 10:26, "If we deliberately keep on sinning after we have received the knowledge of the truth, no sacrifice for sins is left, but only a fearful expectation of judgment and of raging fire that will consume the enemies of God."

This is the Word of God and God does not violate His Word. At one time the Lord was always so near to you, but now because of your sin He is so distant from you. The Lord has come to you many times reminding you to repent of the sins that you are involved in. That is the Holy Spirit telling you to turn back to Jesus - before it is too late. Even now the Holy Spirit is speaking to you to turn away from sin and to come back to Jesus. Pray the following prayer:

"Lord Jesus, forgive me. I have sinned against you. I repent of all sin. Cleanse me from all sin and wash me in your precious Blood. I have been so unworthy. Help me to overcome all sin."

Be absolutely honest with God. Do whatever it takes to come back in obedience to God. As John the Baptist said: "produce fruit in keeping with repentance", Luke 3:8. This act may involve a cost. However, whatever cost is involved, it is nothing compared to being eternally condemned to Hell. If you are living in sin with someone break up with them immediately. If you are getting drunk and high with your buddies, stop going out with them altogether. You CAN say no to sin. Whatever God commands you to do, He empowers you to do.

"If your hand causes you to sin, cut it off. It is better for you to enter life maimed than with two hands to go into Hell, where the fire never goes out. And if your foot causes you to sin, cut it off. It is better for you to enter life crippled than to have two feet and be thrown into Hell. And if your eye causes you to sin, pluck it out. It is better for you to enter the kingdom of God with one eye than to have two eyes and be thrown into Hell, where 'their worm does not die, and the fire is not quenched.' " Mark 9:43-48.

I now present one more part of the divine revelation God gave Mary K. Baxter. This is also very relevant to the subject of this book.

- Beginning of Excerpt, From "Divine Revelation Of Hell", by Mary K. Baxter-

A Prophecy From Jesus to All.

Jesus said, "These things are now beginning in the earth, are yet to be, and are soon coming upon all the earth. The fiery serpent is part of the beast. These prophecies you are about to read are true. The revelations are true. Watch and pray. Love one another. Keep yourselves holy. Keep your hands clean.

"Husbands, love your wives as Christ loved the church. Husbands and wives, love each other as I have loved you. I ordained marriage and blessed it with My Word. Keep the marriage bed holy. Cleanse yourself from all unrighteousness and be pure, even as I am pure.

"The holy people of God have been led away by flatterers. Do not be deceived; God is not mocked. Understanding will come to you if you will open your ears and listen to Me. This is the Lord's message to the churches. Beware of false prophets who stand in My holy place and deceive with flatteries. Oh earth, My holy people have fallen asleep to the sound of false doctrine. Awake, Awake! I tell you that all unrighteousness is sin. Cleanse yourself from all sin of the flesh and the spirit.

"My holy prophets lived holy lives, but you have rebelled against Me and My holiness. You have brought evil upon yourself. You have sinned and brought yourself into bondage to sickness and death. You have committed iniquity and have done wickedly and have rebelled against Me. You have departed from My precepts and from My judgments. You have not hearkened to the words of My servants, the prophet and the prophetess. Curses instead of blessings have come upon you, and still you refuse to return to me and repent of your sins.

"If you will return and repent and if you will honor Me with the fruit of righteousness, I will bless your homes and honor your marriage beds. If you will humble yourselves and call upon Me, I will hear you and bless you.

"Listen, you ministers of My Holy Word. Do not teach My people to sin against their God. Remember that judgment begins at the house of God; unless you repent, I will remove you for the sins you have taught My people. Do you think that I am blind that I cannot see and deaf that I cannot hear?

"You who hold the truth in unrighteousness and line your pockets with silver and gold at the expense of the poor - repent, I say, before it is too late. On the day of judgment you will stand alone before Me to give an account of what you did with My Holy Word. If you call upon Me in repentance, I will remove the curse from your lands and bless you with a mighty blessing. If you will repent and be ashamed of your sins, I will have mercy and compassion on you, and I will not remember your sins anymore. Pray that you may be an overcomer.

"Awake to life and live. Repent to the people you have led astray and taught false doctrine. Tell them you have sinned and that you have scattered My sheep. Repent to them.

..."Again I tell you, do not defile the marriage bed. Do not defile the body in which the Holy Ghost dwells. Sins of the body lead to sins of the spirit. Keep the marriage bed holy. I made man for woman and woman for man and decreed that the two should be united in holy matrimony. Again, I say awake."

- End Of Baxter Excerpt-

If you are a minister that has in the past promoted false doctrine - and as you can see in this book "Once Saved Always Saved" is one of those false doctrines - then take heed to what Jesus is telling you in this prophecy. If there is any sin in your life repent of that first before trying to figure out what all these scriptures about falling away really mean. Sin is very deceptive and if you are under its sway, then satan has a wide open door to keep deceiving you and enslaving you into his seductive doctrines.

Take special note of Jesus' instructions in the above prophecy, "Awake to life and live. Repent to the people you have led astray and taught false doctrine. Tell them you have sinned and that you have scattered My sheep. Repent to them."

And keep in mind that ministers and teachers of God's word are judged much more strictly. As James 3:1 says, "Not many of you should presume to be teachers, my brothers, because you know that we who teach will be judged more strictly." Make very, very

75

certain that what you teach regarding salvation and what you teach about falling away is in line with ALL of God's Word. Pray earnestly to God that He correct you in those areas where you are wrong. Pray like you never have before. Study God's Word like you never have before. And believe when God shows and reveals things to you about this subject. And again if there is any sin in your life - repent of it. Otherwise, satan is going to lead you into greater and greater deception.

CHAPTER 7

NAMES CAN BE ERASED FROM
THE LAMB'S BOOK OF LIFE

As you know, one's name must be found in the Book of Life at the Great White Throne Judgment, Revelations 20:11-15, if one is to escape the sentence of the lake of fire - which is the second death. The greater question though, for those who have received Christ in the past, and the question we will seek to answer in this chapter is: "Once one has been saved and his name has been recorded in the Book of Life, is it possible for his name to be erased or removed from the heavenly record?"

The overwhelming biblical evidence is that such a possibility **does** indeed exist. One scripture that bears considerable weight on this subject, is the message of the Lord Jesus Christ to the church of Sardis:

Revelation 3:5. "He who overcomes shall thus be clothed in white garments; and I will not erase his name from the book of life, and I will confess his name before My Father, and before his angels."

The Lord's promise here is clearly conditional. If one is to avoid being "erased" from the "book of life," Jesus taught that it is imperative that he "overcomes." Scripture teaches that the true children of God are those that obey God and overcome the world, "For everyone born of God overcomes the world.", 1 John 5:4a. Recall also 1 John 3:10a, "This is how we know who the children of God are and who the children of the devil are: Anyone who does not do what is right is not a child of God."

The context of Jesus' words to the church of Sardis as well as a host of other passages prove the fact that not all believers, by their own choice, automatically and inevitably overcome. The church of Sardis was filled with many compromisers, Revelations 3:1-3, but only a few overcomers, Revelations 3:4. The Lord's glorious promise not to erase the overcomers names from the book of life to those in Sardis, also served as a solemn warning to the compromisers in Sardis. Jesus warned the backsliders - those who deliberately kept on sinning - in Sardis who had at one time "received and heard," that they needed to take His warning seriously and repent or else He would come upon them "like a thief" and it would be too late:

"Remember therefore what you have received and heard; and keep it and repent. If therefore you will not wake up, I will come like a thief, and you will not know at what hour I will come upon you." Revelations 3:3.

Here we see that Jesus does not promise the compromisers in Sardis that He will not erase their names. Rather He warns them that if they refuse to wake up He will return to them as a thief. Notice that this was a very serious warning. Recall how, Jesus often warned His disciples to be ready for His return, for He would come back as a thief to all who were **not** prepared to meet Him. This means that they may very well die in their unrepentant state without any chance of repentance to get right with God again - and such would be condemned to Hell, Matthew 24:42-51, Luke 12:35-48, 1 Thessalonians 5:1-5, Revelations 3:3, Revelations 16:15.

One can confirm that Hell is indeed the judgment by recalling the scriptures that Jesus gave in the gospels when He spoke of returning "as a thief." According to Jesus Himself, "returning as a thief" means sudden destruction and damnation. The relevant passage is in Matthew 24:42-44,48-51 where it states:

"Therefore keep watch, because you do not know on what day your Lord will come. But understand this: If the owner of the house had known at what time of night the thief was coming, he would have kept watch and would not have let his house be broken into. So you also must be ready, because the Son of Man will come at an hour when you do not expect him. . But suppose that servant is wicked and says to himself, `My master is staying away a long time,' and he then begins to beat his fellow servants and to eat and drink with drunkards. The master of that servant will come on a day when he does not expect him and at an hour he is not aware of. He will cut him to pieces and assign him a place, in Hell, with the hypocrites, where there will be weeping and gnashing of teeth." Matthew 24:42-44,48-51.

Notice very carefully that those that Christ comes upon "like a thief" will be assigned a place in Hell, "He will cut him to pieces and assign him a place, in Hell, with the hypocrites, where there will be weeping and gnashing of teeth."

A similiar passage is in Luke 12:35-48: Be dressed ready for service and keep your lamps burning, like men waiting for their master to return from a wedding banquet, so That when he comes and knocks they can immediately open the door for him. It will be good for those servants whose master finds them watching when he comes. I tell you the truth, he will dress himself to serve, will have them recline at the table and will come and wait on them. It will be good for those servants whose master finds them ready, even if he comes in the second or third watch of the night.

But understand this: If the owner of the house had known at what hour the thief was coming, he would not have let his house be broken into. You also must be ready, because the Son of Man will come at an hour when you do not expect him."

Peter asked, "Lord, are you telling this parable to us, or to everyone?"

The Lord answered, "Who then is the faithful and wise manager, whom the master puts in charge of his servants to give them their food allowance at the proper time? It will be good for that servant whom the master finds doing so when he returns. I tell you the truth, he will put him in charge of all his possessions.

But suppose the servant says to himself, `My master is taking a long time in coming,' and he then begins to beat the menservants and maidservants and to eat and drink and get drunk. The master of that servant will come on a day when he does not expect him and at an hour he is not aware of. He will cut him to pieces and assign him a place with the unbelievers. "That servant who knows his master's will and does not get ready or does not do what his master wants will be beaten with many blows. But the one who does not know and does things deserving punishment will be beaten with few blows. From everyone who has been given much, much will be demanded; and from the one who has been entrusted with much, much more will be asked.", Luke 12:35-48.

Again, carefully notice that Jesus was addressing His servants - those who have genuinely believed. Everyone who "knows his master's will." He was warning **believers** about falling away and getting entangled back into the sinful ways of the world.

Jesus, after rebuking the compromisers in the church at Sardis, encourages the overcomers in the church of Sardis "But you have a few people in Sardis who have not soiled their garments; and they will walk with me in white; for they are worthy", Revelations 3:4. From all this, we see that overcomers must remain loyal, "stay awake," and "keep" their "garments" clean, lest Christ return to them as a thief: "Behold, I am coming like a thief. Blessed is the one who stays awake and keeps his garments, lest he walk about naked and men see his shame." Revelations 16:15. Many in the church of Sardis had backslidden and rather than "staying awake" dozed off into spiritual death; rather than keeping their garments clean, they were soiling them in the sin and filth of the world, Revelations 3:1-3.

One cannot "stay awake" unless he has first been made awake! One cannot begin to "keep" his garments unless he has first been given garments to keep! This proves that these warnings were, and are, to previously genuine believers who fell back into spiritual death and, since they were not overcoming, were having their names erased from the Book of Life. Revelations 3:5 leaves no other possibility. Those who were compromising and soiling their garments were being erased from the Book of Life and their destination, in their unrepentant state, was now eternal Hell.

It is in the context of these warnings about returning "as a thief" that Jesus promises that He will not erase the names of the overcomers from the Book of Life, Revelations 3:5. From this we see that the obvious condition to remaining in the Book, according to the Lord Jesus Christ, is overcoming obedient faith. Obviously those in Sardis who had soiled their garments, could not be considered overcomers and so they were being erased from the Book of Life. Jesus' intent was that they would recognize their spiritually DEAD, prodigal, condition in His church and repent.

Because of its serious implications, let us keep looking at Revelations 3:5. Quote: "he who overcomes. I will not erase his name from the book of life." Unquote. This is a solemn and tremendous claim. The very same finger of Christ that writes, is the very same finger that can erase, a name from the Book of Life. It is wise to take special note of the plain and solemn implication that your name will be struck out of that Book - if you deliberately keep on sinning and keep soiling your garments. The words of Jesus in Revelations 3:5, as well as Hebrews 10:26-31, 2 Peter 2:20-21, and many others, are much too plain to be neglected or misunderstood.

It is possible that a name, like the name of a dishonest official, can be struck off the rolls. Do not let unbelief or the distractions of this world blind you or deceive you from that fact. Take it into account in your daily life. It is possible for a man to "cast away his confidence", Hebrews 10:35. It is possible for him to make a shipwreck of his faith, 1 Tim. 1:19. And, if your name is not in the Lamb's Book of Life, then at the moment of your death you will be cast into eternal Hell.

My dear ex-brethren, I wish, I really wish, I could accurately call you brethren. Oh how I wish it. But I cannot and neither can Jesus call you His own anymore because of your willful deliberate sinning against Him. It is only the overcomers whose names are kept upon the roll. Those soiled people at Sardis had a name to live by and obey, and they thought their names were in the book of life. But when they died and the Book was opened: Behold! A Blot! Their names were not there!

Likewise, what a shock it will be for millions of disobedient professing Christians at the Great White Throne Judgment who were taught that they need not be overly concerned about Jesus' words in regard to overcoming as they could never really be blotted out of the book of life. What a shock it will be for multitudes, that have been lulled into a false sense of security believing that no matter how much they soiled their spiritual garments their names would remain in the Book of Life. What a shock it will be as the fatal illusion to which they had succumbed is shattered as they hear Christ's words echo throughout the judgment hall, "Depart from me, accursed ones, into the eternal fire which has been prepared for the devil and his angels", Matthew 25:41b.

Again, I realize this all sounds very fearful, but if you deliberately persist in your sin, the reality is that God's **promises** of judgment truly are to be greatly feared. For it states in Isaiah 8:12-13, "The Lord Almighty is the One you are to regard as Holy, He is the One you are to fear, He is the One you are to dread.", Isaiah 8:12-13.

As you have seen, warnings against forsaking God's kingdom for the kingdom of the world are found throughout scripture. Scripture teaches that if we love the world, we shall perish along with the world, 1 John 2:15-17. Paul tells us that Demas who was one of his "fellow workers" in the Lord, Phil 24, Col. 4:14, forsook him having loved this present world, 2 Tim. 4:10. God further warns us that believers who forsake their first love for the world become spiritual "adulteresses" and "makes himself an enemy of God", James 4:4. The scriptures make it abundantly clear that one cannot serve sin and hence satan, the "god of this world," and the true and living God at the same time, Matthew 6:24, 12:30, 1 Corinthians 10:21.

The scriptures warn, those who profess Christ yet deliberately keep on sinning, of spiritual death, Hebrews 10:26-31, 2 Peter 2:20-21. Jesus promised "Truly, truly, I say to you, if anyone keeps My word he shall never see death . If anyone keeps My word, he shall never taste of death", John 8:51, 52b. Note that this promise is only for the one who "keeps" His "word," not for those who love their sin and deliberately keep on sinning. The scriptures are clear that deliberate sinners experience spiritual death, Luke 15:24, 32, Romans 8:12-13, 1 Timothy 5:6, 11-12, 15, Hebrews 10:26-31, Hebrews 12:9, James 5:19-20, 1 John 5:16.

This truth is especially significant to our study, as those who were failing to overcome in the church of Sardis, and thus were having their names blotted out of the "book of life," are described by Jesus as those who "are dead", Revelations 3:1, and "about to die", Revelations 3:2. Thus the "book of life" contains the names of those who have been given life in Christ by God's grace and have their citizenship in Heaven. Those forsaking Christ, His word, His grace and His kingdom will experience spiritual death and have their names "blotted out" of the "book of life."

The scriptures are clear that THOSE WHO PRACTICE SIN AND REFUSE TO REPENT WILL NOT INHERIT THE KINGDOM OF GOD, 1 Corinthians 6:9-10, Eph. 5:1-8, Gal. 5:16-21, 6:7-9, Revelations 21:7-8. By refusing to repent they refuse to have their sins cleansed by the precious Blood of the Lord Jesus Christ. And without the Blood of Jesus there is no salvation.

Do not seek to gain the world at the expense of your very soul, Luke 9:23-27. "See to it that you do not come short of the grace of God." Do not exchange your heavenly "birthright" for the "deceitfulness of sin", Hebrews 12:14-16, 3:6, 12-14. Truly repent from all sin and thereafter keep your garments white as snow through living obedient faith in the cleansing Blood of the Lamb, Revelations 3:4, 16:15, 22:14-15. Pray seriously and sincerely to God, and follow up with action, that He instill a real fear of God into your heart. Pray that you may become an overcomer in the faith and not a compromiser with the world, that you may rejoice in Christ's promise now and at the final judgment.

In spite of Revelations 3:5 some still believe and state that God never erases names from the book of life. The fatal flaw of this thinking is not only the fact that it has no biblical support, but that it is clearly contradicted by scripture. As we shall see, the perfectly Holy God most certainly does erase names from the book of life! In Exodus Ch. 32 we see that after Moses had ascended the Mount to receive the ten commandments he returned to find the children of Israel in a grave state of idolatry as they danced and worshipped the golden calf so soon after the Lord had delivered them from Egypt. This was a "great sin", Exodus 32:30-31, and for starters three thousand people were immediately put to death, Exodus 32:28. Subsequent to three thousand people being wiped out Moses began to make intercession for the people, praying:

"Alas, this people has committed a great sin, and they have made a god of gold for themselves. But now, if thou wilt forgive their sin - and if not, please blot me out from thy book which thou hast written!" Exodus 32:31a-32.

First of all let it be noted that Moses evidently **did** believe that names could and would be blotted out of the book of life and offered the blotting of his name on behalf of his people. Now notice that the Lord does NOT tell Moses that: "He never blots anyone's name from His book of life." On the contrary, the Lord emphatically states just the opposite:

"AND THE LORD SAID TO MOSES, WHOEVER HAS SINNED AGAINST ME, I WILL BLOT HIM OUT OF MY BOOK but go now, lead the people where I told you. Behold, my angel shall go before you; nevertheless in the day when I punish, I will punish them for their sin." Exodus 32:33-34.

To hold or promote the idea that "God never erases a name from His book of life" in the face of God's very own declarations affirming the opposite is extremely fatal and rebellious thinking, and to teach such a doctrine to others is unconscionable. So serious was their idolatry that God promised to BLOT THEIR NAMES FROM HIS BOOK !

In the New Testament, Christians are warned to not be deceived about the fact that idolaters would **not** inherit the kingdom of God, 1 Corinthians 6:9-10. "Do you not know that the wicked will not inherit the kingdom of God? Do not be deceived: Neither the sexually immoral nor IDOLATERS nor adulterers nor male prostitutes nor homosexual offenders nor thieves nor the greedy nor drunkards nor slanderers nor swindlers will inherit the kingdom of God." 1 Corinthians 6:9-10.

As you can see, the scriptures state clearly that idolaters will go to the lake of fire. "But the cowardly, the unbelieving, the vile, the murderers, the sexually immoral, those who practice magic arts, the IDOLATERS and all liars - their place will be in the fiery lake of burning sulfur. This is the second death.", Revelations 21:8.

No wonder the beloved apostle John closes his first epistle warning believers, "Little children, guard yourselves from idols", 1 John 5:21. Let us guard ourselves from the idols of this age. Let us keep in mind that such Old Testament judgments were recorded in the scripture as "examples" to warn us new covenant believers, of the judgment we will face if we turn away from the living God to the idols of sin and wickedness, 1 Corinthians 10:1-13. If you fantasize and like to get involved in your sin - that my reader is your idol - which you love above God, even though He so loved you and sacrificed for you.

Contrary to what some are teaching, Jesus did not say you can get away with anything and "I'll never erase you out of My book." Christ taught that the one "who overcomes . I will not erase his name from the book of life, and I will confess his name before My Father, and before his angels." Revelations 3:5.

To those who deliberately keep on sinning, as Hebrews 10:26-31 describes, I solemnly submit the following warning. It is very direct and strongly worded. But I tell you this not because I hate you but because I love you. If you were driving off a cliff unawares I would scream and yell at the top of my voice to warn you. Please receive this warning in that spirit:

If you insist on sinning and not repenting and if you die in that state, then at the Great White Throne Judgment you will find that, contrary to what some deceived teachers are promoting, Jesus' words as written in the Bible will prevail. How shocked you will be when you learn too late the truth about the consequences of your wickedness. How shocked you will be when you learn that, contrary to the popular seductive lie that "nothing" you could possibly do, and "under no circumstances" could you forfeit your place in the Book of Life, you discover to your own eternal loss and dismay, that you have been totally deceived, and stricken from the Book.

What weeping and gnashing of the teeth will abound when you learn the horrible news that you were totally deceived when you bought into the lie that you could continue in sin and still be saved, and find out that you have lost your very soul forever - without hope, without mercy, and with the eternal realization that you will suffer in Hell without end. And all of this because you loved your sin over and above God your loving Creator, His Son Jesus who suffered a horrible death on the cross for you, and the Holy Spirit who repeatedly called and tried so desperately to bring you back to the Lord.

As you are reading this message you probably sense danger in your heart. That sense of danger is the "Fear of the Lord" and it is essential in guiding you back to the ways of the Lord. Don't reject it. Thank God that He is still working in your heart to believe. For the Fear of the Lord is the beginning of wisdom. But I must forewarn you that unless you allow that understanding lead you to true repentance toward the Lord, then the enemy will come in later and steal this word from your heart. It is **extremely** dangerous to cast away the solemn warnings from the Lord. And believe me, as the days and weeks go by, the tendency will be to forget and hence reject "the Fear of the Lord" from your heart. But if you do cast away God's gracious warnings away from you, and continue in your sin, then your heart will become harder and harder as time goes on. And remember death can happen at any time. There truly is no guarantee that you will live even one more day.

One of the things that I know about sin is that if you continue to think and act upon it, your spiritual sensitivity to God will keep getting duller and duller until you hardly sense God at all in your life. God is still there at times trying to get you to repent of sin and to turn back to Him but it is very soft because of sin's dulling effect on your conscience.

I will relate to you a true story. I remember once when I was in college. I would use an alarm clock, a very loud one, to wake me up. I always "intended" to wake up early. There was a time, however, when I would ignore the alarm clock. The first few days the alarm clock would ring, loudly. I did awake and turn off the alarm clock and went back to sleep. Then in later days I did awake but then I did not even bother turning off the alarm - I simply went back to sleep. Throughout all these times I always intended to "wake up." But I didn't follow through on my intentions. In still the next few days I did the same thing - the alarm went off and I awoke - I heard the alarm - but again I ignored it, did not turn it off, and went back to sleep. Eventually, I got to the point where the alarm came on, and remember it was a loud alarm, but I didn't even hear it anymore, and it didn't even wake me up anymore! I became insensitive to the loud alarm clock!

This is exactly the way sin operates in your life. If you keep thinking after and committing sin and ignoring God's voice calling out to you to turn away from those sins, and to turn to Him, then eventually you get to the point where you become insensitive to God's voice. Basically your conscience is seared and is not able to sense the evil and destructive nature of the sin you are involved in.

Yes, you can continue in sin and rebellion against God and risk that your life may not end in the near future. But what if it does? You may find yourself in Hell forever. And once you are there - you are forever doomed in severe eternal painful torment. In pain more excruciating than being burned alive. This is not a comfortable subject, I know, but it is better for you to know about this now - when you can do something about it - rather than later, in Hell, where you will never be able to get out.

This message you now have in your hand is a "very load alarm clock" being given to you so that you can wake up. What will you do now that God has so graciously provided you this message? Please don't turn off, ignore, or sleep through this alarm. Take it to heart. Repent of your sins now - now that the alarm is loud and clear upon your spiritual ears. For surely when the weeks go on and your memory gets further away from this message, will you awake when the alarm is thereby relatively silent? If you don't repent now when this message is so strong on your mind, what would cause you to repent later when this message is much duller on your memory? This is the very reason that the Word of God says in Hebrews 3:7,8a, "So, as the Holy Spirit says: 'Today, if you hear His voice, do not harden your hearts.' "

Please do not turn away from this message. As Hebrews 3:12 says, "See to it, brothers, that none of you has a sinful, unbelieving heart that turns away from the living God." If you ignore this message by not repenting now, you are essentially turning away from this message and thereby turning away from the living God. Don't do this. Please don't do this. Turn back to Jesus now. He loves you so dearly. Even though you have backslidden, Jesus still loves you and wants you back. Please repent and turn back to Jesus. He desires so much to forgive you and restore you.

"Remember therefore what you have received and heard; and keep it and repent. If therefore you will not wake up, I will come like a thief, and you will not know at what hour I will come upon you. But you have a few people in Sardis who have not soiled their garments; and they will walk with me in white; for they are worthy. He who overcomes shall thus be clothed in white garments; and I will not erase his name from the book of life, and I will confess his name before My Father, and before his angels. He who has an ear, let him hear what the Spirit says to the churches.", Revelations 3:3-6.

CHAPTER 8

HELL, LUST, AND PORNOGRAPHY

There are three resources from which we all pull doctrinal beliefs:

1) our imagination;

2) what someone told us; or

3) the Word of God (the Bible).

Since God never lies and is never in error, we must all rely on the Word of God over and above what our imagination tells us or what someone else tells us. Even if the Word of God contradicts everything we have ever been taught by our minister or churches we must put God's Word before everything. As it says in Romans 3:4, "Let God be true, and every man a liar."

As uncomfortable as it is to some, we all need to give heartfelt warnings to those who profess to be Christians about the eternal danger of sexual immorality.

Before getting into this, let me explain a couple of terms which Jesus and the apostle Paul taught about salvation and about who would and would not go to heaven.

The Term WICKED :

The first term we will look at is the term WICKED. To understand what the term WICKED means let us look at 5 scriptures (there are hundreds more but these should suffice):

"Now the men of Sodom were WICKED and were sinning greatly against the LORD." Genesis 13:13

"The WICKED will not stand in the judgment, nor sinners in the assembly of the righteous." Psalm 1:5

"You are not a God who takes pleasure in evil; with you the WICKED cannot dwell." Psalm 5:4

"Salvation is far from the WICKED" Psalm 119:155

"This is how it will be at the end of the age. The angels will come and separate the WICKED from the righteous and throw them into the fiery furnace, where there will be weeping and gnashing of teeth." Matthew 13:49-50

As you can see, in the Bible, the term WICKED always refers to those who are enemies of God, those who are separated from God - - that is those who are not saved and who go to Hell if they die without repenting.

The Term INHERIT :

The next term we will look at is the term INHERIT. According to Jesus, salvation or eternal life is INHERITed :

"And everyone who has left houses or brothers or sisters or father or mother or children or fields for my sake will receive a hundred times as much and will INHERIT eternal life. Matthew 19:29 (NIV)

In Hebrews 1:14, salvation is also referred to as being INHERITed: "Are not all angels ministering spirits sent to serve those who will INHERIT salvation?" Hebrews 1:14 (NIV)

Jesus also refers to INHERITing eternal life in John 4:14 and Revelation 21:6-7.

In John 4:14, Jesus refers to eternal life as a "spring of water welling up to eternal life" : "Whoever drinks the water I give him will never thirst. Indeed, the water I give him will become in him a spring of water welling up to eternal life." John 4:14 (NIV)

In Revelation 21:6-7, Jesus also uses the term "spring of the water of life" to refer to eternal life or salvation:

"6 It is done. I am the Alpha and the Omega, the Beginning and the End. To him who is thirsty I will give to drink without cost from the spring of the water of life." 7 "He who overcomes will INHERIT all this, and I will be his God and he will be My son."

Rev 21:6-7 (NIV)

That Jesus is referring to salvation or eternal life is also confirmed by the phrase "and he will be My son" in verse 7.

Notice also in verse 7 the word INHERIT, and that eternal life (the spring of the water of life) is what is being INHERITed: "He who overcomes will INHERIT all this." In this page of scripture Jesus is specifically referring to eternal life as what is being INHERITed. This is also consistent with what Jesus stated in Mat 19:29: "And everyone who has left houses or brothers [etc.].. for my sake will.. INHERIT eternal life." - Matthew 19:29

Eternal Life: Who INHERITs It And Who Does Not

Let Us Now Read All Of Revelation 21:5-8 :

5 He who was seated on the throne said, "I am making everything new!" Then he said, "Write this down, for these words are trustworthy and true." 6 He said to me: "It is done. I am the Alpha and the Omega, the Beginning and the End. To him who is thirsty I will give to drink without cost from the spring of the water of life. 7 He who overcomes will INHERIT all this, and I will be his God and he will be My son.

8 But the cowardly, the unbelieving, the vile, the murderers, the sexually immoral, those who practice magic arts [witchcraft], the idolaters and all liars -- their place will be in the fiery lake of burning sulfur. This is the second death." Rev 21:5-8 (NIV)

In contrast to those who INHERIT eternal life, in verse 8, Jesus mentions those who will not INHERIT eternal life. Notice that THE UNBELIEVING ARE NOT THE ONLY ONES BEING CONDEMNED TO HELL. In addition to the unbelieving there is also, "the cowardly [those who deny Christ], the vile, the murderers, the SEXUALLY IMMORAL, etc... their place will be in the fiery lake of burning sulfur." (I emphasize the grievous sin of sexual immorality because it is such a prevalent sin in our day and age -- even by many who profess to be Christians.)

91

Jesus makes no distinction as to whether these sinful people were previously saved or not. In fact, He makes it a point to include the UNBELIEVING as only one class of people who are being condemned to Hell.

Notice that when John was addressing believers he stated: "Anyone who hates his brother is a murderer, and you know that no murderer has eternal life in him." (1 John 3:15)

Notice the phrase "NO MURDERER HAS ETERNAL LIFE IN HIM." Since according to Jesus in Rev 21:8 the sexually immoral person will meet with the same fate as the murderer then we can also say that, NO SEXUALLY IMMORAL PERSON HAS ETERNAL LIFE IN HIM.

There are not two kinds of murderers -- saved and unsaved. There are not two kinds of witches -- saved and unsaved. There are not two kinds of sexually immoral people -- saved and unsaved. According to Jesus in Rev 21:8, all the cowardly are unsaved, all the unbelieving are unsaved, all the vile are unsaved, all the murderers are unsaved, all the sexually immoral are unsaved, all those who practice magic arts (pharmacia) are unsaved, all the idolaters are unsaved, and all liars (in greek "false ones" – as in false teachers, false prophets, false brethren, etc.) are unsaved. And they will all end up in Hell, unless they genuinely repent in this life and come (or come back) to Jesus.

Notice also that taking illicit drugs to get high (in greek pharmacia) is part of practicing magic arts and is also condemned as worthy of Hell fire.

Similarly, in 1 Cor 6:9-10 Paul states: "Do you not know that the WICKED will not INHERIT the kingdom of God? Do not be deceived: Neither the sexually immoral nor idolaters nor adulterers nor male prostitutes nor homosexuals nor thieves nor the greedy nor drunkards nor slanderers nor swindlers will INHERIT the kingdom of God." 1 Corinthians 6:9-10

The term WICKED has already been explained. The term INHERIT has also. This scripture is another confirmation of what Jesus said in Rev 21:5-8. As you can see the terms and meanings here are very clear, direct, and sound. If you choose to doubt -- you do so in clear contradiction to the word of God.

Notice that the pages Rev 21:5-8 and 1 Cor 6:9-10 are parallel scriptures. Both are referring to salvation and both use the term INHERIT to refer to those who will or will not make it to the kingdom of God.

I realize that very few preach on these pages of scriptures but God's word stands forever. God is faithful and His words cannot and it will not be altered: "I will not violate my covenant or alter what my lips have uttered." Psalm 89:34

Jesus began the Rev 21:5-8 page by saying in verse 5: "Write this down, for these words are TRUSTWORTHY and TRUE." Jesus was emphasizing this page of scripture so that we would all be forewarned of the ETERNAL danger of transgressing into these grievous sins. Jesus does not give idle warnings and He does not exaggerate. He gives us clear and specific words and phrases so that we will know what the truth is. Notice again in Rev 21:8 , "the SEXUALLY IMMORAL .. their place will be in the FIERY LAKE OF BURNING SULFUR."

As hard as it is for some to believe, GOD WILL SEND THE SEXUALLY IMMORAL TO HELL -- even those who once came to Jesus in the past but now went back into the pollutions of the world.

There are many popular even evangelical ministers telling people that their sinning -- even gross evil sins such as murder, and adultery, etc, will not send them to Hell. It is the same thing satan told Adam and Eve. " 'You will not surely die,' the serpent said to the woman." Genesis 3:4

According to Jesus, not only will the UNBELIEVING end up in Hell, the SEXUALLY IMMORAL will also end up in Hell (as will the

93

cowardly, the vile, the murderers, etc.) -- whether or not they were previously saved or not.

According to the Bible the following people are classified as SEXUALLY IMMORAL:

1. Fornicator -- An unmarried person having with someone else who is not married. (Gal 5:19, KJV)

2. Adulterer -- A married person having with someone other than their lawfully wedded spouse. Also an unmarried person having with someone who is married. (Gal 5:19, KJV)

3. Homosexual -- Someone who is having with a person of the same gender. (1 Cor 6:10, Jude 1:7)

4. Bestiality -- Someone having with an animal. (Lev 18:23)

Those who are living together but are not lawfully married are committing the sin of fornication. Although our present day culture may condone this sin, God does not and will not approve of this sin. This sin will send you to Hell as Jesus tells us in Rev 21:8. As already explained, this is true even if you gave your life to Jesus in the past but are now in sexual immorality.

In Luke 13:3 Jesus says "unless you repent you will likewise perish." If you are living with someone who is not your lawfully wedded spouse or if you have been indulging in sex outside of marriage then you are sexually immoral and God will have to condemn you to Hell if you die in that state. But God is not interested in sending you to Hell. God is calling you to repent from your sin -- even if you gave your life to Jesus in the past.

If this describes you, you must do 2 things:

1. Confess your sin to Jesus and ask Him to forgive you.

2. Repent of your sin by permanently leaving the partner or partners you have been having sex with.

If you don't truly repent then confession is worthless. You are merely giving lip service and it is an abomination to God. I realize that what I am saying here is very direct and stern but I want there to be no doubt about the decision and the consequence you are facing. I counsel you to believe God and repent -- or face eternal torment in Hell when you die. And you can die on any day. You are free to choose. But you are not free to choose the consequence of your choice. And according to Jesus, the consequence of a sexually immoral life is eternal torment in Hell.

Believe God -- He does not lie.

THE SIN OF LUST AND PORNOGRAPHY

Note: The first 5 pages in this chapter is based on Dan Corner's article: http://www.evangelicaloutreach.org/lust.htm

(Used by Permission)

In the Sermon on the Mount, the Lord Jesus must have shocked the people of His day when He equated lust to ADULTERY! His actual words from Matthew chapter 5 verses 28 and 29 are:

"But I tell you that anyone who looks at a woman lustfully has already committed ADULTERY with her in his heart. If your right eye causes you to sin, gouge it out and throw it away. It is better for you to lose one part of your body than for your whole body to be thrown into HELL."

Please note the serious consequence of lust or mental adultery. Immediately after verse 28 where Jesus equates lust to adultery He describes the consequence in verse 29. And the consequence is Hell itself. According to Jesus, who always tells the truth, if you lust you will end up in Hell ! Therefore, this sin must not be taken lightly, as many people do.

The chief aim of this article is to provide the facts regarding "lust" as used in Matthew 5:28. Many downplay the serious consequences of lust. Similarly, remember this: Temptation in itself is not a sin. Jesus was tempted, yet Jesus never sinned. Therefore, temptation is not a sin. It only becomes a sin when you yield to it.

The Greek word rendered "lustfully" in Matthew 5:28, NIV, is found elsewhere and translated in such a way as to help us know what the Lord equated to mental adultery. This same exact word is found in Luke 15:16 and Luke 16:21. It is also significant to note that Jesus gave us these other usages. Hence, he chose to use the same exact word in these other teachings as he chose to use in Matthew 5:28! Those verses translate lustfully as longed and longing, respectively:

"He the Prodigal longed to fill his stomach with the pods that the pigs were eating, but no one gave him anything." "And Lazarus was longing to eat what fell from the rich man's table. Even the dogs came and licked his sores." The facts surrounding the sad circumstances of the Prodigal and Lazarus, two other places where Jesus also used the word rendered "lustfully" as mentioned in Matthew 5:28, help us to better understand its meaning.

Regarding its usage by the Lord in Luke's gospel, it seems evident that this word carries a meaning with it that makes it much deeper than just a casual glance at a woman, as some wrongly think. To substantiate this, Strong's Concordance defines this word as "to set the heart upon, i.e. long for". Greek Dictionary, page 31, number 1937.

Near the end of preparing this book, the Holy Spirit prompted me to explain a little more on the meaning of lust. Usually we think that only sexual fantasies qualify as lust. But the phrase "long for" is revealing more about what lust is about. Following the lead provided by Strong's Concordance, I referred to a thesaurus and found that other words synonymous with lust are: longing, desire, covet, wish, yearn, hunger, crave, ache, and pine. If you are longing for, desire, covet, wish, yearn, hunger, crave, ache, or pine for someone who is not your lawful spouse then that my reader is lust. When examining your heart please consider these additional words and test your heart to see if you have any of these sinful desires toward someone who is not your spouse.

When men lust they tend to emphasize the visual and physical aspects of the woman and hunger and crave for a woman that is not their lawful wife. When women lust they tend more to the emotional aspects of desiring, coveting, yearning, or pining for a man that is not their lawful husband.

Again, a casual glance at the opposite sex is not being referred to in Matthew 5:28. However, when actual lust does occur, that is, when one "longs for" another, then adultery is actually committed! To deny this teaching is to doubt God's Word and the Lordship of Jesus Christ! This also clearly refutes the statement I've often heard - "It's okay to look, meaning lust, but not to touch." Jesus never taught lust was okay! Nowhere is this form of adultery, though solely mental, less serious than other forms, although many treat it as such! Remember, Jesus said it can send one to Hell. Matthew 5:29 !

How awesome to ponder this fact in regard to all of the pornographic literature and media that can be found in this country, through magazines, movies, CD's, the internet, and even on TV. Mental adultery is rampant! Truly, this is an "adulterous generation," as Jesus said.

Men committing mental adultery should also be a sobering thought for women who profess to be Christian and desire to please the Lord. Paul wrote that women are to dress "modestly". 1 Timothy 2:9. Yet at the same time, Paul was a grace teacher in the truest sense. So this isn't "legalistic" as some accuse, but simple obedience! To disregard the way you dress might possibly cause someone to stumble into adultery! The same applies to a man and his dress, for women can lust too. Read what Jesus said in Matthew 18:6 about stumbling another into sin and think soberly about the consequences of greater judgment when you cause someone else to sin! Furthermore, a woman who dresses with the intent to make men lust after her is on a par with a prostitute!

In our generation, TV is the prime way people commit mental adultery. Sometimes even while watching news one can be exposed to spiritually unwholesome scenes which the devil is pleased to present. These spiritual pollutants flood into homes across our land. Then people wonder why they are having trouble with lust! It may very well be that more adultery is committed before the TV set than anywhere else!

Furthermore, it's a sad day when people who profess to be God's servants are ensnared by their TV as their precious free time is spent never to be regained! Our generation will have to account for this incredible waste of time at the Judgment. Please note I mentioned "our generation" since television has only been available commercially since just after World War II. TV as a means of distraction and temptation, is something which the Twelve disciples never had. Remember this: Before the invention of TV, Christians got along fine without ever watching it! You can too! Or at least you can reduce the amount of time wasted by being careful and only watching wholesome content. By reducing TV time you will have much more time to labor for the Kingdom in one form or another besides the other advantages of not being tempted to lust or adopt the world's values in the first place.

If you are having trouble with lust or know someone who is, the remedy, in part, is to cut off the source of temptation! It's that simple. If literature is the temptation, then stop going near it. If it's TV or movies, stop watching them. This is what you are to STOP doing. Paul wrote: "Clothe yourselves with the Lord Jesus Christ, and do not think about how to gratify the desires of the sinful nature" Romans 13:14 . Also, remember sinful desires such as lust, adultery are warring against your soul, 1 Peter 2:11. You must war back or be conquered. A fight is a fight and not a "bed of roses"!

Furthermore, to get victory over lust, you should START spending more time with the Lord in prayer and in the Bible meditating on and memorizing certain verses! Hiding God's word in your heart can help stop those mental temptations. The writer of Psalm 119 both prayed and hid God's word in his heart so he would not sin against God: "Do not let me stray from your commands. I have hidden your word in my heart that I might not sin against you". Psalm 119:10,11. We all need to humbly follow this example.

In summary, victory over sin is not just what you do but also what you don't do! In other words, starve your sinful nature by not thinking about how to gratify it and feed your spirit with God's word by meditating in Scripture. Your voluntary thoughts, that is, the thoughts you choose to ponder when free to think about anything you want, are extremely important. Romans 8:5 says, "Those who live according to the sinful nature have their minds set on what that nature desires; but those who live in accordance with the Spirit have their minds set on what the Spirit desires."

Paul wrote, "The one who sows to please his sinful nature, from that nature will reap destruction; the one who sows to please the Spirit, from the Spirit will reap eternal life". Galatians 6:8. Notice that to reap destruction is the opposite of reaping eternal life. In other words, reaping destruction is reaping eternal death or Hell.

In the Old Testament, we also read of lust in passages like Proverbs 6:25-26: "Do not lust in your heart after her beauty or let her captivate you with her eyes, for the prostitute reduces you to a loaf of bread, and the adulteress preys upon your very life." Again, lust leads to destruction and Hell! Therefore, do not take this sin lightly.

By the way, the word rendered "lustfully" in Matthew 5:28 is used in a good sense in 1 Timothy 3:1 and Hebrews 6:11. This latter verse reads: "We want each of you to show this same diligence to the very end, in order to make your hope sure."

Paul emphasized free-will and human responsibility. He did this without contradicting his own grace message. He wrote, "Keep yourself pure". 1 Timothy 5:22. Undoubtedly, many will have to make MAJOR TV changes to obey this command! Victory over TV will benefit you and others in this life and throughout eternity, but get ready for the battle regarding it!

Job was the most unique man on earth in his day - being blameless, upright, a man that feared God and shunned evil. Job 1:8. This man said of himself, "I made a covenant with my eyes not to look lustfully at a girl". Job 31:1. This is also very important in our day in light of Matthew 5:28-29 and the rampancy of pornographic literature, movies and commercials in our vile country.

Paul wrote, "Put to death, therefore, whatever belongs to your earthly nature: sexual immorality, impurity, lust, evil desires and greed, which is idolatry". Colossians 3:5 . Please note: it's your responsibility coupled with the power of God. Romans 8:13. that is the victory over lust.

It might surprise some to learn that Jesus used the word from which we get our word "pornography" in Revelation 22:15, which the King James Version translates as whoremongers. In the greek the original word is pornos. From which we get the word pornography. The N-I-V bible translates the word as sexually immoral, and stated that along with some others, such are "outside" the city of New Jerusalem or Heaven. If we compare Revelation 21:8 to this same verse, we know their specific location is clearly the lake of fire!

Someone, who calls himself alex271, sent me the following testimony about the struggle they had with sexual immorality, and specifically about how God warned him about pornography and how that it would send him to the lake of fire.

- Beginning of alex271 Testimony -

I know how pleasurable sin can be. Even though I was married, I used to lust after a woman at work, I used to fantasize about her. And even masturbated for hours fantasizing about her. I admit, it was pleasurable. I also lusted after other woman as well. I also looked at pornography and lusted after some of those beautiful women and masturbated while looking at those naked women.

Hey, I was a sinner on my way to Hell just like many of you. But God got my attention and even spoke to me one day after I had been viewing some pornography and was on my way to go masturbate in a bathroom. He simply told me without anger in His voice :

"WHOREMONGERS, SHALL HAVE THEIR PART IN THE LAKE WHICH BURNETH WITH FIRE AND BRIMSTONE."

This statement He actually spoke to me right after I viewed some pornography and on my way to go masturbate. What is worse at the time I went ahead and masturbated - even after God spoke this bible phrase to me.

At first I was wondering. Why is God telling me this? I even thought He was not referring to me. That is how deceitful sin actually is. In the midst of it - you don't think you are guilty of it. It really is amazing how deceitful our hearts can be. Even when we know the scriptures.

Again the exact phrase God spoke to me and in a very clear voice was:

"WHOREMONGERS, SHALL HAVE THEIR PART IN THE LAKE WHICH BURNETH WITH FIRE AND BRIMSTONE."

The statement that God spoke to me is part of a verse in the bible, in Revelation 21:8, King James Version which says, "But the fearful, and unbelieving, and the abominable, and murderers, and whoremongers, and sorcerers, and idolaters, and all liars, shall have their part in the lake which burneth with fire and brimstone: which is the second death."

This showed me that pornography, lust, and masturbation will definitely send me to Hell. Later I finally repented of this lust and adultery of my heart and I turned to Jesus with all my heart. It took a while but with God's help I was finally able to overcome and learned how to keep pure. Don't despair. If you really want to overcome God will help you. Just don't play games with God. God hates that.

Having done the same types of sins that many of you have done and are doing, I cannot condemn you or judge you. I definitely do not think I am better than anyone else.

I just know with all my heart that all people who get involved in sexual immorality in any form will end up in Hell as God warns - unless they repent. Repent means to turn away from sin and totally give your life to Jesus. This I know because God never lies to us. Also God doesn't want any of us to go to Hell.

Remember: God's warning in Revelation 21:8.

WHOREMONGERS, SHALL HAVE THEIR PART IN THE LAKE WHICH BURNETH WITH FIRE AND BRIMSTONE.

Going to Hell forever is not worth the temporary pleasures of sin. It's just not worth it.

- End of alex271 Testimony -

In still another testimony the following was sent to me by someone who visited my website at, realityofhell.weebly.com. The person identified himself as luap123311. I will use luap for short. explains how he had a dream that his late father was in torment in Hell - and that what landed him there was his love of pornography.

- Beginning of luap Testimony -

Luap.   October 6, 2010.

God has taken me to the " Lake of Fire " on two occasions and I saw that it is a Lake that is made of Field Stones and I saw a soul in the Lake trying to escape? but it could not and I saw rise and fall back into it - and the soul had Black Eyes - and I was really terrified to see someone there. I ask God to reveal who that soul was - so God gave another dream and I saw my father. His love to pornography got him there and there is nothing that I can do to help him. Now he will suffer for Eternity !

The next week luap wrote the following:

Luap.   October 12, 2010.

My father took us to church every week but I guess he did not listen to the Gospels where Jesus Christ said if we Lust after a woman we have already fornicated with her. So - pornography that my father enjoyed brought him Eternal Damnation forever. Jesus means what he says!

- End of luap's Testimony -

So we see here another illustration that, Pornography and Lust WILL send you to Hell. Remember and believe what Jesus says in Revelation 21:8 about all forms of sexual immorality also called whoremongering, including adultery, fornication which is sex outside of marriage, lust, pornography which is lust and adultery of the heart, homosexuality, bestiality (sex with animals), and all other forms of sexual immorality:

"WHOREMONGERS, SHALL HAVE THEIR PART IN THE LAKE WHICH BURNETH WITH FIRE AND BRIMSTONE"

Jesus does not lie. He will render judgment precisely as He warns. He will be sad and cry for you but He will still have to send you to Hell if you persist in sin and do not repent.

In yet another testimony, Jesus gave visions of Hell and Heaven to Pastor Yong-Doo Kim from Korea, some of his relatives, and some of the people in his church. The following is some excerpts from their testimonies.

- Beginning of Pastor Kim's Testimony -

Excerpts from the Book. Baptize by Blazing Fire. by Pastor Yong-Doo Kim. (Free website download. Used by permission from spiritlessons.com)

Pastors and Church members committing adultery

My heart aches whenever ministers make headline news and their dirty secrets are exposed on TV. I would either turn the TV off or shred the newspaper in fear of my family getting wind of it. As a minister, I am very ashamed and embarrassed. I am bewildered, I do not know what I should do. I feel as though it is me being exposed since I am also a minister. I have no desire to discuss or expose the dirty hidden secrets of the other fallen ministers. However, the Lord had pressed me to record the details in this book.

Jesus commanded that we never commit the sin of adultery. Among the countless of people going to Hell, many of them are adulterers. The Lord had reminded us, "Didn't your church members witness the adulterers tormenting in Hell? Adultery is a sin that is very difficult to repent." The Lord hates His people committing spiritual adultery but He also despises people committing physical adultery even more.

Many ministers and church members are deluded in thinking that if they just confess their sins using the name of Jesus, they are absolutely forgiven. As a result, they continue to commit the same sin, repent again and think they are covered by grace. They trample on grace and do not hesitate to commit the same adulterous sin over and over. The Lord resented their delusion. Revelation 2:21-23. Before a person comes to Jesus, they do evil out of ignorance. Jesus is very angry that people have accepted Him as their Lord, but continue to sin repeatedly without hesitation. The Lord shouted angrily, "It will be very difficult to forgive ministers who commit adultery in secret. If they do not repent sincerely, they will end up in Hell!"

I compassionately pleaded, "Lord! They are human beings, they are flesh, therefore, they could still fall and make mistakes, right? If a person dies, he or she will not have the opportunity to repent. But while they are alive, won't they be forgiven if they repent? There are many verses in the bible that states that You will forgive, if one repents." The Lord replied, "the ministers know the scriptures very well, and yet if they commit adultery, they will be harshly judged. It will be difficult for them to be forgiven!" The Lord austerely reproved me.

I persistently pleaded to the Lord for mercy and refused to back down. I pleaded like Abraham did. "Lord! Although you are right, if you send them to Hell for their past sins without forgiveness, it would seem unfair. Among that group, there are probably some who have lead many souls to You. There are probably some ministers who are leading their church in a pleasing way. Are not some like this in the group of adulterers?" The Lord fearfully rebuked me, "As a Pastor, do you not know your scripture?" Jesus helped me remember Philippians 2:12, "continue to work out your salvation with fear and trembling."

Although the Lord had rebuked me, I continued to debate and argue with Him. "My beloved Lord! But those ministers have sacrificed their whole life for you. They have spent their time on earth to serve You. Don't You think You should give them opportunities to repent? If I claim that Pastors go to Hell, who would believe me?"

There was a moment of silence and pause. The Lord then quietly and with dignity spoke. "God the Father agrees with Me. If the ministers who have committed adultery sincerely repent with fear, they shall be forgiven. But if they turn back to their wicked ways and commit the same sin after repentance, they will be mocking God! It will not matter whether they have lead small or mega ministries or have lead great or weak ministries, they will have committed the sin in which God hates the most. You will have to bear that in mind."

Then, in a vision, the Lord showed me a specific pastor who fell in love with a young sister in his church. They often met to have sexual relations. Eventually, their affair was exposed to the Pastor's wife. She was in such shock that her stress level was greatly elevated and even dangerous. The wife attempted to persuade the Pastor to repent, but he would not listen. The wife could no longer endure the pain and shock, so she became very depressed. Then, she committed suicide, a choice unbelievers make. Now she's in Hell and in great torment.

The Lord said, "Whenever I see that daughter, my heart is torn apart. How can I not send that Pastor to Hell? That Pastor is still in ministry. His repentance was not genuine. Even today, he is living a life of delusion and self deceived. His way of thinking is corrupt. No one can ever deceive me. No one can ever cover up the truth with lies!"

Blotting out names from the Book of Life

There once was a deaconess in our church. When she was living faithfully, she received many gifts from the Holy Spirit. However, the gifts were all taken back. Soon afterward, she began drinking and smoking frequently. Moreover, she would talk to a man over the telephone daily, and meet him in secret. I persistently attempted to persuade her from dating that man. I even yelled at her but she continued to see the man. God is patient with people. However, if people do not repent, they will be subject to His wrath. God showed me in a vision that He had erased her name from the book of life. When we found out, we all shook in fear.

When God gives us a chance, we must take it, no matter what. Jesus said, "That particular saint mocked God, and troubled the Holy Spirit. Therefore, if she does not mourn and sincerely repent, she will not be entering Heaven. If the judgment of the congregation members is hard, then how much more will I judge the Pastors who are committing adultery? The ministers must repent to the point of death. Currently, the ministers of today are mocking God, they say, 'these are the days of grace, and the gospel sets us free, just repent and one will be forgiven unconditionally!' These are the days one needs to be in fear more than the days of the old testament." The Lord warned us that the day is coming when we will all have to give account for our deeds.

As I write on this chapter, I am experiencing many hours of dismay and dissension. Jesus said, "Do we then nullify the law by this faith. Not at all! Rather we uphold the law." Romans 3:31. In fact, we are living our daily life within the Lord's amazing grace. However, living in His grace does not mean our sins just disappear. We are abusing God's grace if we do not repent. A daily repentant life is the fastest and shortest route to God's mercy and compassion.

- End of Pastor Kim's Testimony -

Notice in this testimony that the deaconess, at one time was a good obedient Christian. But when she backslid into sin, she caused her name to be erased from the book of life. This really should scare the Hell out of us. In Revelation 3:3-5, Jesus mentions that if one is not victorious over sin, then their names will be blotted out of the book of life.

In the bible, Jesus says: "So remember what you have received and heard; and keep it, and repent. Therefore if you do not wake up, I will come like a thief, and you will not know at what hour I will come to you. But you have a few people in Sardis who have not soiled their garments; and they will walk with Me in white, for they are worthy. He who overcomes will thus be clothed in white garments; and I will not erase his name from the book of life, and I will confess his name before My Father and before His angels."

Because of its serious implications, let us keep looking at Revelation 3:5. For *"he who overcomes - I will not erase his name from the book of life."* This is a solemn and tremendous claim. The very same finger of Christ that writes, is the very same finger that can erase, a name from the Book of Life. It is wise to take special note of the plain and solemn implication that your name will be struck out of that Book - if you deliberately keep on sinning and keep soiling your garments. The words of Jesus in Revelation 3:5, as well as Hebrews 10:26-31, and 2 Peter 2:20-21, and many others, are much too plain to be neglected or misunderstood. It is possible that your name can be struck off the rolls. Do not let unbelief or the distractions of this world blind you or deceive you from that fact. Take it into account in your daily life. It is possible for a man to *"cast away his confidence"*, Hebrews 10:35. It is possible for him to make a shipwreck of his faith, 1 Timothy 1:19. And, if your name is not in the Lamb's Book of Life, then at the moment of your death you will be cast into eternal Hell.

Notice also how Jesus states that His grace cannot be trampled on, and that repeated sinning is mocking God and that true repentance must involve repenting to the point of death. In other words, God's grace is not a license to sin. In Jude 1:4 God's Word states: "For certain individuals whose condemnation was written about long ago have secretly slipped in among you. They are ungodly people, who pervert the grace of our God into a license for immorality and deny Jesus Christ our only Sovereign and Lord."

If we repeatedly sin over and over and only repent on the surface, even when we confess our sins, and ask for forgiveness, but then go back to sinning over and over again. Then our repentance is not genuine. And we are essentially treating God's grace as a license to sin. As seen in Pastor Kim's testimony, in these cases, Jesus is saying that this is mocking God. And as it says in Galatians 6:7, "Do not be deceived: God cannot be mocked. A man reaps what he sows." And in the case of lust, pornography, adultery, having sex outside of marriage, and in all forms of sexual immorality, what you reap is eternal torment in Hell itself.

As Jesus says, we must repent to the point of death and not repeat the sin. This is genuine repentance. Then and then only will God forgive you. Forgiveness happens only when we truly forsake the sin and do not repeat it. As Proverbs 28:13 states, "But whoever confesses and forsakes his sins will have mercy." To truly repent means to truly forsake the sin. Ask God to help you overcome. He is eager to help you. Do whatever it takes to overcome and stop sinning. If you don't you will forever wish you had after you are in torment in Hell forever. It really is that serious!

In still another scripture, Hebrews 10:26-31, God warns us: If we deliberately keep on sinning after we have received the knowledge of the truth, no sacrifice for sins is left, but only a fearful expectation of judgment and of raging fire that will consume the enemies of God. Anyone who rejected the law of Moses died without mercy on the testimony of two or three witnesses. How much more severely do you think someone deserves to be punished who has trampled the Son of God underfoot, who has treated as an unholy thing the blood of the covenant that sanctified them, and who has insulted the Spirit of grace? For we know Him who said, "It is mine to avenge; I will repay," and again, "The Lord will judge His people." It is a dreadful thing to fall into the hands of the living God.

It is revealing to note that the warning in Hebrews 10:26-31 was addressed to believers. Notice the phrase "the blood of the covenant that sanctified them", showing that the people who are deliberately sinning are those who in the past gave their life to Jesus but now are behaving unfaithfully and wickedly. It is very obvious that the warnings of Revelation 3:5 and Hebrews 10:26 and others are warnings to Christians who are back into a lifestyle of sinning. And the promised judgment for those who do not repent is eternal Hell itself. Since the promised judgment in Hebrews 10:26 is, "a fearful expectation of judgment and raging fire that will consume the enemies of God."

God is deadly serious about His warnings to us about sexual immorality. In another testimony, Doctor Roger Mills describes how Jesus took him to Hell and showed him many things in Hell and several people who are now in Hell's torment, even ministers who came to Christ in the past but lived a life of sexual immorality and other sins.

- Beginning of Testimony by Doctor Roger Mills -

Excerpt from the book: "While out of My Body I Saw God, Hell and the Living Dead" by Doctor Roger Mills.

The Lord God Jesus continued to say, "The souls that you see here this hour are being tormented in the Outer Darkness of Hell. They have been here for a long time. Many years. They are ministers from around the world. They had plenty of time to repent of their hypocritical, unrepentant, sinful, and evil ways, but they did not. I had given them much space to repent, but they only ignored my loving grace. They were warned. They knew what would happen to them if they continued to blaspheme by Holy Word, and live hypocritical."

I looked to the right of me, and I saw a huge shadow racing across the ground. As the shadow came closer to where the Lord God

109

Jesus and I were standing, I got a closer look at it and I realized that I was not looking at a shadow. It was thousands of tiny black spiders. I watched in horror as the spiders raced across the ground in masses, crawling up on the bars to the very top of the jail cells, where the bishops were. I noticed they had teeth and red eyes. I had never seen a spider with teeth before. I watched as they entered the jail cells, and began to crawl all over the bishops, attacking them and biting them all over their bodies with their teeth. There were masses of them; so many that they covered all the cells. You could not see the cells or the poor souls that were in them because thousands of those black spiders covered them like an enormous black blanket. Oh what screams and cries came from within the cells, from the apostles, prophets, teachers, evangelists, pastors, and bishops, who were the disobedient children of God! Then the Lord God Jesus said to me, "These are the cursed ones, the disobedient children that I called into My kingdom, but this hour they are here in this place of outer darkness, tormented and suffering for their disobedience."

Then the Lord God Jesus said, "Look, listen and learn. Those spiders you see are demonic spirits who were assigned by the Prince of Hell to go to Earth and seduce ministers of God. These demonic spiders have the power to cause men and women to be sexually seduced. They are sexual seducing spirits, better known as unclean spirits. They are part of the blame for those preachers that you see in those prison cells to be here this very hour. These preachers became involved in all sorts of fornication: adultery, homosexuality, masturbation, pornography, lust, the ways of Sodom and Gomorrah, sexually taking the advantage of little children and bestiality. Had they repented, gaining control over their sexual appetite, they would not have been here. Only if they had not given heed to those seducing demonic unclean spirits that appear to be spiders. All demon spirits do not look like this. There are different shapes and forms of many sizes."

- End of Testimony by Doctor Roger Mills -

It is very obvious from God's word and these testimonies that God really means what he says in Revelation 21:8 which states that:

The sexually immoral, that is, "WHOREMONGERS SHALL HAVE THEIR PART IN THE LAKE WHICH BURNETH WITH FIRE AND BRIMSTONE."

The Eternal Danger of Lust

What is God's view of how important your sexual life is?

1 Thessalonians 4:6 says, "that no man transgress and wrong his brother in this matter, because the Lord is an avenger in all these things, as we solemnly forewarned you." And in Revelations 22:15 God plainly tells us that: "Outside [of Heaven] are the dogs, those who practice magic arts, the *sexually immoral*, the murderers, the idolaters and everyone who loves and practices falsehood."

This means that the consequences of lust and all forms of sexual immorality including pornography, adultery, sex outside of marriage, are going to be worse than the consequences of mere bodily death. Jesus said, "Do not fear those who kill the body and after that have no more that they can do. But I will warn you whom to fear. Fear him who after he has killed has power to cast into Hell". Luke 12:4-5. In other words God's vengeance is much more fearful than earthly annihilation. And according to 1 Thessalonians 4:6, God's vengeance is coming upon those who disregard the warning against lust.

As previously mentioned, in Matthew 5:28-29 Jesus says, "Every one who looks at a woman lustfully has already committed adultery with her in his heart. If your right eye causes you to sin, pluck it out and throw it away; it is better that you lose one of your members than that your whole body be thrown into Hell." Take careful notice here that Jesus said Heaven and Hell are at stake in what you do with your eyes and with the thoughts of your imagination. Lust will cause, "your whole body to be thrown into Hell."

Again here Jesus says that if you don't fight this sin of lust -- which is adultery of the heart -- with the kind of seriousness that is willing to gouge out your own eye, you will go to Hell and suffer there forever.

There are many professing Christians who have a view of salvation that disconnects it from real life, and that nullifies the warnings of the Bible and puts the sinning person who claims to be a Christian beyond the reach of biblical warnings. And this doctrine is comforting millions on the way to Hell.

Simply stated, Jesus said, if you don't fight lust, you won't go to Heaven. The stakes are much higher than mere physical death.

Justifying Faith Is Sin-Fighting Faith

Are we not, then, saved by faith, by believing in Jesus Christ? We are indeed! Those who persevere in faith shall be saved. How do you lay hold on eternal life? Paul gives the answer in 1 Timothy 6:12, "Fight the good fight of faith: lay hold on eternal life."

Recall also the essential role of faithful obedience as Jesus emphasizes in Matthew 7:21-23, "Not everyone who says to me, 'Lord, Lord,' will enter the kingdom of Heaven, but only the one who does the will of my Father who is in Heaven. Many will say to me on that day, 'Lord, Lord, did we not prophesy in your name and in your name drive out demons and in your name perform many miracles?' Then I will tell them plainly, 'I never knew you. Away from me, you evildoers!' " Real faith is always accompanied with real obedience. You cannot have one without the other.

The Apostasy That Must Be Destroyed

The great apostasy that I am trying to destroy in this message is the deception that says, "faith gets you to Heaven and holiness only gets you rewards." This is the great deception of our day. In Hebrews 12:14 God says, "Without holiness no man shall see the Lord". So according to the bible -- which is God's Word -- not only faith but also holiness, which reveals true faith, are needed to see the Lord and make it to Heaven.

Again in Matthew 7:21 Jesus says, "Not everyone who says to me, 'Lord, Lord,' will enter the kingdom of Heaven, but only the one who does the will of my Father who is in Heaven." Jesus is so clear in his warning about disobedience. If you choose to accept man's word over God's word then you will reap disastrous and eternal consequences. Only God's word can be depended on to be absolutely true.

The battle for obedience is not optional. The battle for obedience is absolutely necessary for salvation because, obedience itself IS the fight of faith. The battle against lust is absolutely necessary for salvation because it is the battle against unbelief. Faith delivers from Hell and that same faith, if genuine, also delivers from lust and from sexual immorality and from Hell. This means if you are in lust or sexual immorality then you are not in faith, and if you are not in faith then you are destined for Hell, unless you repent.

True faith will lead you into holiness and the reward of seeing the Lord in Heaven. But if you persist in lust or sexual immorality in any form and therefore lack holiness, you will not make it to Heaven and you will not see the Lord.

Again, as God says in Hebrews 12:14, "WITHOUT HOLINESS NO MAN SHALL SEE THE LORD".

- Hell Testimony from Dr. Roger Mills -

Excerpt from the book: "While Out Of My Body I Saw God Hell And The Living Dead" by Dr. Roger Mills

In this testimony Jesus gives Dr. Roger Mills a tour of Hell and shows him many people in torment there. In this testimony Jesus is explaining what will happen to sinful Christians who do not repent. Specifically Jesus reveals what happens even to "believers" that commit adultery in their heart.

- Beginning of Testimony by Dr. Roger Mills -

113

"But she that liveth in pleasure is dead while she liveth." 1 Tim 5:6.

The Lord God-Jesus continued to say to me, "I am going to introduce you to some people, and I will let you see them as though they were already living in their future. What I am telling you is this: I will allow you to see and talk to certain people in this very room, all of whom are dead, yet are very much alive on Earth!"

There were many people in this room, and some of them I recognized as preachers! I was shocked to see one preacher in particular that I knew. He was my friend when he was alive on Earth! He did not see me, but I saw him. There were many other people I saw that I knew could not possibly be dead, yet I saw them in the Room of the Future Dead, in Hell. I saw people who I thought would never be there and the ones that I thought would go to Hell, I did not see.

Immediately, I could see through the wall. It appeared as if I were watching a television screen. I saw a jail cell, with rusty black iron bars. The bars ran up from the dirt ceiling and down to the dirt floor. It was a very small cell, and inside, lying on the dirt floor was my brother Randy. I remember him distinctly. I said to the Lord God-Jesus, "I know who that is! That is my oldest brother, Randy!" Then the Lord God-Jesus said to me. "I have brought you here to Hell this hour so that you can see his future. So that you can go back to the Earth and tell him to change and repent from his lukewarm and sinful-Christian lifestyle. If he doesn't repent, he will be here in Hell. Tell him that I know about the many unconfessed and unrepented acts of sin he has committed, and the hurt and pain he has caused his family. I know of his arrogance, I know of his pride and I also know about the pain and hurt that is in his heart."

Immediately I saw two more jail cells that contained my brothers, Michael and Bernard. Jesus gave me the same message for both of them. I asked the Lord God-Jesus, "Where is my brother Tony?" The Lord God-Jesus answered and said, "The demonic spirit named the Prince of Hell assigned demonic creatures to take him as well as your other brothers to their assigned jail cells, where they shall receive their temporary punishments of torment for their unconfessed and unrepented sins. Then on the Final Day of Judgment, I will command that the Prince of Hell release them from their jail cells, and they will be judged for their lukewarm and backslidden-Christian lifestyle. Then they shall be cast into the Lake of Fire, which is the Second Death."

After hearing the Lord God-Jesus say this, I cried bitterly. Then He said, "There is nothing that I can do about it that I haven't already done, but there is something that you can do about it! Go back to the Earth and warn your brothers before it is too late! If they repent, I will have mercy upon them, forgive them and cleanse them from all unrighteousness, but if they don't, great will be their punishment in the Outer Darkness of Hell."

Then the Lord God-Jesus said to me, "Come!" We continued to walk through the Room of the Future Dead. He said," I brought you into this room because I knew that you would appreciate it." The Lord God-Jesus told me to turn around and look. There, sitting approximately five feet before me was a black wooden chair. Sitting on the chair was a image of a person with their back turned toward me. I stared at the image and I knew instantly who it was. I walked over to the chair and looked into the face of that person. Recognizing that it was my best friend, Richard, I yelled at the top of my voice in complete horror, "Richard, what are you doing in this terrible place?!" His response was silence. I put my hand on his shoulders and said, "Talk to me, Richard! What's wrong?" He gave no response, except for his cold, transfixed stare at nothing. I continued to ask him over and over again, "What's wrong? Talk to me!" Still, I received no response but silence. Just then, an eerie feeling came over me. It was as though I could feel his emotions, and those I perceived were that of rage and hate. I noticed that now, when I looked into his face, his countenance changed.

In thought I said, "This doesn't look like the Richard I know." He did not seem to be the same person that I knew back on the Earth. At one time, joy and peace radiated from his face. Now hate, bitterness and meanness dominated his facial expression - even his eyes. I became frightened.

Just then, the Lord God-Jesus said to me, "Look, listen and learn. I have brought you here to this Room of Outer Darkness in Hell to see your friend Richard as he really is." The Lord God-Jesus knew that I was confused at what I had just heard him say about Richard because the Richard that I had always known was loving, sensitive and compassionate. The person sitting in that chair was not him.

The Lord God-Jesus continued to say, "As I have told you before, I am the Alpha and the Omega; the beginning and the end and the first and the last. I can show anyone his or her past and future. I allowed you to see a small portion of Richard's future. He has died and come here to Hell. While he was yet on Earth, he lived another life that you knew nothing about. He was an adulterer and he lusted in his heart for women; sexual perversion polluted his heart. He began to tell lies, and at moments of rage, profanities would issue from his mouth. I came to him on many occasions by my Spirit and convicted him of his wrongdoings. He knew that he was doing wrong, but at certain times he just stopped caring to correct himself.

Marital problems, along with other problems, began to invade his life. The more that I tried to love him and warn him, the more stubborn and rebellious he became, until one day, Satan killed him in a car wreck and brought him here to Hell. He became angry, mean and bitter about being here. Immediately, I came to him and he asked me why he was in Hell. He said to me, "I am a Christian. I am a member of the Church. I have done long work for you, Lord." Then I said to him, "You know the reason why you are here. I have pleaded with you to repent of your sins, especially the adultery. You stopped for a while, but the lust and adultery in your heart grew worse later on. You knew and read what it says in my word about adultery." Exodus 20:14, "Thou shall not commit adultery." Matthew 5:27-28, "Ye have heard that it was said by them of old time, THOU SHALT NOT COMMIT ADULTERY: But I say unto you, That whosoever looketh on a woman to lust after her hath committed adultery with her already in his heart."

Then the Lord God-Jesus continued to say that Richard had told Him that he had changed, and pleaded with Him to let him out. The Lord God-Jesus explained, "I said to him, 'I was not the cause for you to be here. I never sent you to Hell and I can't let you out.' " Richard having heard that, walked away very slowly and with much anger. I began to cry, and I said to the Lord God-Jesus, "What is going to happen to him?" The Lord God-Jesus said, "Soon, evil spirits will come for him, and throw him into a cell and torment him, right up to the time of the great throne judgment."

"Please let him out! Let him out!" I said. The Lord said to me, "I did not send him to Hell. He sent himself. Neither is it my decision to let him out. There is nothing that I can do for him that I have not already done. However, there is something that you can do. That is why I have brought you here. I want you to go back to the Earth and tell him everything that I showed you and allowed you to hear. Tell him that I love him, and I want him to repent."

After hearing the Lord God-Jesus say that, I knew that there was a chance Richard may not die and come to Hell. I felt a little relief, but my heart was still heavy. I was depressed and frightened as we continued to journey through the Outer Darkness of Hell. In the Room of the Future Dead, I also saw many relatives of mine, but in particular I saw my dad. I called out to him, but there was no response. I tried desperately to find him, but trying to find him was like looking for a needle in a haystack. He quickly disappeared amongst the thousands of people that were in that room. I knew then that it was just a matter of time – that he would die soon. I had a chance to go back to the earth and reach him before it was too late.

- End of Hell Testimony from Dr. Roger Mills -

Knowing how prevalent the sin of lust, pornography, and masturbation is among men, and woman too, I also present the following which is a very helpful article from, Into The Light Ministries. (Free website download.)

The title of the article is:

A 12 Letter Dirty Word: Masturbation.

http://www.intothelight.org/masturbation.asp

This article is from a single Christian males perspective, however the principles are the same for both men and women, married or not.

This is a subject that no one wants to talk about. Mainly because most of us are guilty of it and continue to be or have been guilty of it in the past.

We will cover four things that have to be established on this subject and we will cover them one at a time.

Question 1. Is masturbation a sin?

By the Word of God yes it is.

Question 2. How bad is it?

We know there are no degrees to sin. It's like a woman saying I am a little bit pregnant. She either is or she isn't. If she is that baby is going to grow. That may be a bad metaphor but if you let sin go, it will grow, and it will give birth to death not life.

Question 3. How wide spread is it?

Question 4. How do we stop, repent and turn away from it?

Is masturbation a sin and if so how bad is it? The first clue should be why would God convict you of it if it weren't sin? Why after masturbating do you feel guilty and empty?

1st Corinthians chapter six verse eighteen: "Shun immorality and all sexual looseness, flee from impurity in thought, word or deed. Any other sin which a man commits is one outside the body, but he who commits sexual immorality sins against his own body." Amplified Version.

Matthew chapter five verse twenty eight: Jesus said "But I say to you that everyone who so much as looks at a woman with evil desire, that is lust, for her has already committed adultery with her in his heart."

Guys I don't care what woman or women you are thinking about when you masturbate, if they are married or not or just made up. The fact is your thoughts are impure and the deed is too. God's Word commands us to shun and flee from these thoughts, not dwell on and use them. You may say that nice and toned down term it's just 'self-sex'. God says you are in adultery and fornication. It is sin.

1st Corinthians chapter six verses nineteen and twenty: "Do you not know that your body is the temple, the very sanctuary, of the Holy Spirit Who lives within you, whom you have received, as a gift, from God? You are not your own, you were bought with a price, purchased with a preciousness and paid for, made His own. So then, honor God and bring glory to Him in your body."

Matthew chapter twelve verse thirty five: "The good man from his inner good treasure flings forth good things, and the evil man out of his inner evil storehouse flings forth evil things."

James chapter one verses thirteen thru fifteen. "Let no one say when he is tempted, I am tempted from God; for God is incapable of being tempted by, what is, evil and He Himself tempts no one. But every person is tempted when he is drawn away, enticed and baited by his own evil desire, that is lust and passions. Then the evil desire, when it has conceived, gives birth to sin, and sin, when it is fully matured, brings forth death."

That evil passion to masturbate is yours and yours alone it is an evil desire in your heart. If you are born again and you being the very temple of Almighty God, decide to drag Him through it. In all your fantasies and thoughts you bring God along, is it any wonder He is grieved? It is sin.

Sex was a gift from God for a married couple to give of themselves to each other. Masturbation is selfishness pure and simple. It is sin.

You a man are having sex with you a man, what's that called; I don't care what you are thinking of. You, a man, are performing a physical act with you a man. It is sin.

Romans chapter twelve verse one: "I APPEAL to you therefore, brethren, and beg of you in view of, all, the mercies of God, to make a decisive dedication of your bodies, presenting all your members and faculties, as a living sacrifice, holy, devoted and consecrated, and well pleasing to God, which is your reasonable, rational, intelligent, service and spiritual worship."

When you masturbate you do none of these, you do just the opposite. It is sin.

How bad is it? It is a grievous sin and it will grow and bring forth death.

How wide spread is it? Jesus said the last days would be as the days of Noah and Sodom. Luke 17:26-29.

Some of these statistics are as much as twelve years old and some have to do with pornography. Men you know what you do when you look at porn. In a 1994 survey of 600 Christian men. Of the married men who responded 61% said they masturbated, with 82% saying they did it at least once a week. 96% of single men under the age of 20 admitted to a masturbation habit. Only 23% gave "enjoyment" as a reason for doing it. The rest said "from habit," "because of their sex drive," "they were addicted to it," or from "lack of an outlet for sex" as the reason they engaged in masturbation.

In his book, "Men's Secret Wars", Patrick Means reveals a confidential survey of evangelical pastors and church lay leaders. 64% of these Christian leaders confirm that they are struggling with sexual addiction or sexual compulsion including, but not limited to use of pornography, compulsive masturbation, or secret sexual activity.

A study of university networks by Palisades Systems found searches for child pornography at 230 colleges nationwide. The research revealed that 42% of all searches on the file-to-file sharing systems involved child or adult pornography. The study also found that 73% of movie searches were for pornography, 24% of image searches were for child pornography, and only 3% of the searches did not involve pornography or copyrighted materials.

In December of 2000, the National Coalition to Protect Children and Families surveyed 5 Christian Campuses to see how the next generation of believers was doing with sexual purity:

48% of males admitted to current porn use 68% of males said they intentionally viewed a sexually explicit site at the school. From MSNBC Survey 2000: 60% of all website visits are sexual in nature.

At 13.3 billion dollars, the 2006 revenues of the sex and porn industry in the U.S. are bigger than the NFL, NBA and Major League Baseball combined. Worldwide sex industry sales for 2006 are reported to be 97 billion dollars.

To put this in perspective, Microsoft, who sells the operating system used on most of the computers in the world, in addition to other software, reported sales of only 44.8 billion dollars in 2006. Internet Filter Review. Just one more identifier if you are still wondering if we are in the days of Sodom and Gomorrah.

The number one search term used at search engine sited is the word "sex". Users searched for "sex" more than any other terms such as "games," travel," "music," "jokes," "cars," "weather," "health," and "jobs" combined. The study also found that "pornography and porno" was the fourth-most searched for subject. From Alexa Research.

When I was a kid I would try to sneak a look at playboy magazines. Now we have it piped into our homes by cable, by dish, by the Internet. We can even download it on our phones. We don't have to look on the street as in the days of Sodom; it's in our homes and it's in the church.

How widespread is masturbation? It is rampant everywhere, in the church and in the world and all the sin, the porn, child porn, prostitution that blossoms from it.

Do you think that the girls that are in the porn industry enjoy it?

"Most girls who enter the porn industry do one video and quit. The experience is so painful, horrifying, embarrassing, humiliating for them that they never do it again." Luke Ford, quoted by CBS News.

Now think about this. Hollywood currently releases 11,000 adult movies per year - more that 20 times the mainstream movie production, films that you can view at you local cinema. LA Times Magazine, 2002. In an average porn movie there are between 5 and 20 girls that's between 55,000 and 220,000 girls as young as they can get them to be used and scared this way a year. These are just the legal ones not counting the one made with minors or children. That is just in the U.S.

God is going to hold you personally responsible for your sin of masturbation if you do not repent. But you are every bit as guilty of sin as those girls that got lured in to doing a movie. You are every bit as guilty as the producers of that movie that lured them into it. Why? You gave them your money to buy them. You helped make those producers rich, rich enough to lure those young girls with the money or a quick fix; you gave them the money every time you rented a movie. Are you so foolish and I am talking to Christian men, are you so foolish that you think God is going to punish those producers, send them to Hell and just let you slid on by when you supported it. Just because you wanted to masturbate? Just so you could get your selfish, ungodly two-minute high.

The average time a porn movie is watched in a hotel room is 12 minutes. Time dot com. March 29, 2005.

1st Corinthians chapter six verse nine: "Do you not know that the unrighteous and the wrongdoers will not inherit or have any share in the kingdom of God? Do not be deceived, misled: neither the impure and immoral, nor idolaters, nor adulterers, nor those who participate in homosexuality."

Masturbation is sexual immorality. Jesus said that sexual immorality will take you to Hell. The fruit of it is that it has help build a multi billion-dollar industry that has helped to destroy millions of lives. Keep practicing this sin and stand before Jesus with any excuse you wish. Gods Word says the sexual immoral will not enter in but will be cast into the lake of fire.

How do we stop, repent and turn from it? God has delivered me from pot, cocaine, crystal, acid, speed and alcohol. With each of these came a battle. Of all of these and some of these drugs I did for decades. The sin of masturbation was the biggest battle. But if you say that God can't deliver you for any reason, it's too strong or that's the way I'm made, if you give any reason stating that God can't deliver you of this sin you have: 1. Just called Almighty God a liar. 2. Just proved you don't want to be delivered.

1st Corinthians chapter ten verse thirteen: "For no temptation, no trail regarded as enticing to sin, no matter how it comes or where it leads, has overtaken you and laid hold of you that is not common to man. That is, no temptation or trail has come to you that is beyond human resistance and that is not adjusted and adapted and belonging to human experience, and such as man can bear. But God is faithful to His Word and to His compassionate nature, and He can be trusted not to let you be temped and tried and assayed beyond your ability and strength of resistance and power to endure, but with temptation He will always also provide the way out, the means of escape to a landing place, that you may be capable and strong and powerful to bear up under it patiently."

Jesus took all our sin indeed the sin of the whole world upon the cross. He came to set us free that we might live a holy and pleasing life toward God. Those who are set free by the Son of God are free indeed. God is faithful and He can be trusted, He will let no temptation come to you that is beyond your ability to resist and endure.

1st Thessalonians chapter four verses three and four: "FOR THIS IS THE WILL OF GOD, that you should be consecrated, separated and set apart for pure and holy living: that you should abstain and shrink from ALL sexual vice, that each one of you should know how to possess, control, manage, his own body in consecration, that is purity, separated from things profane, and honor."

It is God's will that you live a life free from sexual sin. A life of pureness and holiness in thought and deed. He would not require this of you if He knew you could not do it. He does not call you to build a house without giving you the tools, skill and materials to do it.

You still have to do the labor and it can be hard work. The question is, are you willing to do what it takes?

You first have to come to realize how deadly serious this sin is. It was easy for me to say I know I was a drunk and a drug addict. God said no drunkards shall inherit the Kingdom of God. When something has that much control over you, you know it.

I first had to realize it was a sin not a disease. That would mean that I was in danger of going to Hell because I was sick. I did not catch drunkenness like I would catch the flu.

It was because of my actions and lack of actions, choices I made that led me to depend on alcohol and drugs to deal with my life and myself.

It is the same with masturbation. Yes God gave you a sex drive. Yes God made women attractive. Yes God gave most men a desire to have that one companion to be intimate with in all areas of life and not just sexually. That is why God gave us marriage.

Paul wrote that he wished that all men were like he himself single or unmarried. But this was a gift from God for him to fulfill his calling that the Lord had placed upon is life. 1st Corinthians 7: 7-9. Most men and I believe most women do not have that gift. At the same time God clearly states that we are not to walk in any sexual sin. Sex is a gift that is not to be opened until you are married, sex is a gift that He gave to bless a husband and wife not us singles. Yes, God gave me a sex drive and I thank God He did, but it is not my master, Jesus is.

Here is part of the key, is Jesus your Lord? Are you subject to His will and not to your own?

When I went to God seeking deliverance from drinking it never happened. I could not understand why. I begged God but alcohol was my master. I sought Christ to get a problem out of my life. I did not give up my life to get Christ's life. It was I that lived not Christ Jesus that lived in me.

When I finally realized that masturbating was every bit as damming as being a drug addict, and had just as much control of me, and was just as destructive to me and those around me, just as grievous to my Lord and Savior who died for me that I could be free, it was then that I saw what I had to do. I had to go; I had to die, so Jesus could have that area of my life and **live** through that area of my life.

When I started to seek God just to know Him more, just to draw closer to Him, and know and love the One who made me, He began to show me why I drank and took drugs. God is a loving Father and He wants to remove anything that separates Him from His children. He started to show me the roots of the problem were as I had always focused on the fruit of the tree. He then helped me pull up the roots and the tree died.

It is the same with masturbation don't go seeking God just to get rid of the problem. Don't seek God just to get something from Him, seek Him to get to know Him. He knows it is a serious problem and He wants you free of it more than you do. If you are truly born again from above, you are a part of His body. He wants to impart His life in you. He may show you a lot of roots you will have to pull. There may be some things you may have to repent of that you never tied into the question of 'why does this urge to sin win in me?'

There is a major difference between the sin of being a drunk or a drug addict and the sin of masturbation. I did not have a God given desire to get drunk and puke all over. I learned that all on my own. I do have a God given desire to find the woman God has for me and get married. Masturbation is the abuse of that gift. I'm already cheating on my wife and I'm not even married yet. If like Paul I had the gift to be single I would not have that desire at all. Many people say they have that 'gift' but are trying to stamp out the desire when God wanted them to have a wife and they live a lonely miserable life or they secretly sin.

Yes it is a God given desire but His will was never for it to be your master. Here is what I did. First I made a decision to give God all of my life. I thought I had but I had just given Him bits and pieces before I realized what I was doing and grew tired of the 'piece game'. And here is what you must do, you must totally surrender, give it up, and abandon yourself to God. Jesus said, "If a man puts his hand to the plow and looks back he is no longer fit to be my disciple." The more I really got to know Jesus and His character, the more I became determined to let nothing come between us. God and His will became the primary focus of my life. And now it is the only focus of my life.

If I am to marry, that will be great, if I am to remain single, then that will be great too. I asked God to take the desire away. He didn't but I would have been perfectly content if He did.

Let me just put in here that I learned not to care what people think about me. The whisperers, why does he not get married and do this or that? I am not going to stand and give an account to those people I will to Jesus Christ.

I also realized that this sin would take me to Hell. When you deliberately sin you deliberately reject Christ. We do not know the day or the hour or the second of the rapture. Ask yourself what you want to be doing when Jesus returns for His bride without spot or wrinkle. Laying there masturbating was not on my list.

I determined to fight it. It is an abuse of a God given gift. It is abnormal sex. Not only is it grievous to God but you are also teaching yourself abnormal sexual behavior.

It will be a battle, you have trained yourself to get your quick fix every bit as much as drug addict needs a shot or a snort or a hit of his drug. Your flesh will want it. Remember, Gods Word says to walk after the Spirit not the flesh. When the thought or desire first enters your mind the battle is on. If you had an enemy that was trying to kill you and you hear the sound of a bullet entering the chamber of his gun you don't stand in an open field and decide what to do, YOU MOVE, you react, you get to some cover and you get ready to fire back. Someone once said "you can't keep a bird from flying over your head, but you can stop it from making a nest in your hair." You can't stop the thought from entering your mind but you don't have to dwell on it, MOVE.

Take every thought captive to Christ get you mind on God and what He's called you to do. Get under the cover of the Almighty. The flesh may say to you 'I want it, I want it', again and again. And it can be strong, it may the first time you really ever battled your flesh before, if it is, consider it a revelation, now you understand a little better all those scriptures about fighting the flesh, so fight it.

As I said, especially at first, it can be a real battle but it is a real man, a grown up man, a man of God who is in control of his flesh, one who does not let his flesh control and dictate to him. A real man fights, it is trying to kill you, and sin does not show mercy. You are commanded by God to treat it the same way. I don't care if it attacks you so powerfully that at three in the morning you get up and wax your car to get your mind off it, if that still doesn't work buy a bigger car, buy a fleet if you have to but you can not give in.

Quite watching movies and TV. shows with sexual content, any sexual content, quit the books, the magazines.

Romans chapter twelve verse two: "Do not be conformed to this world (this age), [fashioned after and adapted to its external, superficial customs], but be transformed (changed) by the (entire) renewal of your mind [by its new ideals and its new attitude], so you may prove [for yourselves] what is the good and acceptable and perfect will of God, even the thing which is good and acceptable and perfect [in His sight for you]."

Your friends might give you grief and say it's only a PG or R rated movie even 15 year olds go to them. Yaw, they do and look at the fruit.

Your mind is a container; God gives you the power to renew it. If you keep putting trash in it, it is a trash container and all you are doing is giving your enemy more bullets to fire at you. Put Godly things in and it will become a Godly container. Get back to basics. Read Gods Word and fellowship with those that are serious about serving the Lord and not hiding their own sin, confess your sins one to another, bring it to the light, it's the devil who works in the dark. Pray and ask for God to reveal His will for your life and I mean every part of it. Then do it. Jesus said, "Where I am my servant shall be." Not the other way around. Gods has a plan for you He thought up before you were born, get to it. If you want God to reveal more of His will to you, you first have to do what He has already revealed. Why would He show you more of His plan when you have not obeyed what you already know?

Remember its Heaven and Hell serious. Staying in and repeating a known sin is your choice and you are choosing it over God. God will give you the victory but you have to fight the battle.

As you do these things and anything else the Lord may show you the attacks become less fierce and farther apart. But always be prepared. You have to as Paul said "die daily" and Romans chapter six verse eleven and twelve. "Even so consider yourselves also dead to sin and your relation to it broken, but alive to God, living in unbroken fellowship with Him, in Christ Jesus. Let no sin therefore rule as king in your mortal, short-lived, perishable, bodies, to make you yield to its cravings and be subject to its lusts and evil passions."

I have also been asked to write an article on dating and courtship because the next question I usually get from single men is how do I find a wife? If they have read the Word they usually quote 1st Corinthians 7:27 emphasizing the "seek not a wife" part with a pained look on their face.

Dating and courtship is a whole different study and I will write more on this later. But in brief I will share this since masturbating is sin and it's good to know what is not. The gift of sex is for married couples, that they may express in the physical the love God gave them, for each other to be shared between them alone.

First if anyone can find anywhere in the Word of God that dating as we understand it today is scriptural I would like to see it. It is not. That does not mean you can't meet and get to know members of the opposite sex. But the Word is clear that you treat them as sisters.

"Treat older women like mothers and younger women like sisters, in all purity." 1st Timothy 5:2.

Read the in all purity part again. You don't decide you like her and drive off to Lookout point even if she wants to. Trust me you don't want the girl that is willing to break her vow before God and you are doing the same. In fact if you really love and respect her you would never put her in a place where there could be even a hint of sexual immorality. The devil is a liar and the accuser of the Saints he does not care that nothing has happened between you and her. He will slander her and you if you give him the chance. A Godly husband protects his wife; a Godly man protects his sister. He does not take his sister out and then make out with her.

Meeting the lady and getting married is a gift from God every bit as being single such as Paul's gift. When it is time to receive that gift , and God knows when it is time, let Him bring the lady across your path that He has for you. You trust Almighty God with your eternal salvation but you can't trust Him to bring you a mate? God says He will give you the desire of your heart. He can say that because He is the one who gave you the desire in the first place. When it is time, and fortunately for you and her that will be when you are mature enough to take headship for one of His daughters and when it is His will, for God wants godly families, you can pray and He will answer.

But first I would pray that the Lord would reveal to you what it is to be a godly husband and to put you through the refining fire so that you are ready to take that position. The Word states that when you get married you "shall have trouble in the flesh". It is wise and I state this again IT IS WISE to take care of as much of these troubles as you can before you are married. Then I would pray that the Lord would bring her to you. Don't go seeking, looking to see if this or that girl has enough check marks on your perfect wife list. Pray and trust, let God answer your prayer. All good gifts come from above and God loves you and her. Let Him bring you that gift and her let him bring you.

The fruit of meeting her should increase your service for God not distract you from it for two are better than one when it is God's will. When you two meet trust God to let you both know it, and you can pray singly and together as to whether you are meant to be more than just brother and sister. Remember God is Love. Don't try to manufacture it on your own. That is counterfeit, emotional, conditional love and that is why most, over 50% of Christian marriages end in divorce within 5 years. Take the time to let God fill you with His love for her and fill her with His love for you. If she is the one, God will do this whether you are together or apart. When you come to the point where you know it is God's will to marry her and she hears the same from the Lord, then you are ready to make that commitment, that life long covenant together.

A lot of people will say "that is crazy' and that 'our society does not work this way'. 'You are saying God is a matchmaker'. To that I say yea and amen. Societies change but the Lord thy God does not. He is the same yesterday, today and forever. He made the first match and marriage in the beginning and He still does for those who know Him and seek His will.

"And this is the confidence, the assurance, the privilege of boldness, which we have in Him: we are sure that if we ask anything, make any request, according to His will, in agreement with His own plan, He listens to and hears us. And if, since we positively know that He listens to us in whatever we ask, we also know, with settled and absolute knowledge, that we have, granted us as our present possessions, the requests made of Him." 1st John 5:14-15.

End of Article by Into The Light Ministries.

CONCLUSION.

We see from these testimonies and teachings the very serious consequences of sexual immorality, also called whoremongering, in all its forms. This includes lust, pornography, masturbation, adultery, sex outside of marriage, sex with your boyfriend, sex with your girl friend, sex with your fiance', going to topless bars or sex shops, homosexuality, orgies, bestiality or sex with animals, and sexual molestation of children. Unless the sinner repents we see the very serious danger that whoremongers or the sexually immoral are in. Jesus really does mean what He says in Revelation 21:8.

"WHOREMONGERS, SHALL HAVE THEIR PART IN THE LAKE WHICH BURNETH WITH FIRE AND BRIMSTONE".

Further information about Hell can be found at the following website about Hell: hell3.weebly.com

CHAPTER 9

COME BACK TO THE FATHER
WITH ALL YOUR HEART

Jesus sacrificed Himself so that those who believe in Him could be One with Him in the Most Holy Place and become part of the Body of Christ. Jesus so desires that all people would become saved, stay saved, and become One with Him. Jesus suffered so that none of us would have to suffer for our own sins in Hell.

Isaiah 53:4-5. "Surely He took up our infirmities and carried our sorrows, yet we considered him stricken by God, smitten by Him, and afflicted. But He was pierced for our transgressions, He was crushed for our iniquities; the punishment that brought us peace was upon Him, and by His wounds we are healed."

If you truly repent and ask His forgiveness, Jesus will cleanse you and receive you back to Himself with great joy. He wants you back. Jesus sheds tears and longs for you to come back to Him.

COME BACK HOME!

Let us now read the Story of the Prodigal Son in Luke 15:11-32.

"Jesus continued: There was a man who had two sons. The younger one said to his father, `Father, give me my share of the estate.' So he divided his property between them.

Not long after that, the younger son got together all he had, set off for a distant country and there squandered his wealth in wild living. After he had spent everything, there was a severe famine in that whole country, and he began to be in need.

So he went and hired himself out to a citizen of that country, who sent him to his fields to feed pigs. He longed to fill his stomach with the pods that the pigs were eating, but no one gave him anything.

When he came to his senses, he said, `How many of my father's hired men have food to spare, and here I am starving to death! 'I will set out and go back to my father and say to him: Father, I have sinned against Heaven and against you. I am no longer worthy to be called your son; make me like one of your hired men.' So he got up and went to his father.

But while he was still a long way off, his father saw him and was filled with compassion for him; he ran to his son, threw his arms around him and kissed him. The son said to him, `Father, I have sinned against Heaven and against you. I am no longer worthy to be called your son.'

But the father said to his servants, `Quick! Bring the best robe and put it on him. Put a ring on his finger and sandals on his feet. Bring the fattened calf and kill it. Let's have a feast and celebrate. For this son of mine was dead and is alive again; he was lost and is found.' So they began to celebrate.

Meanwhile, the older son was in the field. When he came near the house, he heard music and dancing. So he called one of the servants and asked him what was going on. `Your brother has come,' he replied, `and your father has killed the fattened calf because he has him back safe and sound.'

The older brother became angry and refused to go in. So his father went out and pleaded with him. But he answered his father, `Look! All these years I've been slaving for you and never disobeyed your orders. Yet you never gave me even a young goat so I could celebrate with my friends. But when this son of yours who has squandered your property with prostitutes comes home, you kill the fattened calf for him!'

`My son,' the father said, `you are always with me, and everything I have is yours. But we had to celebrate and be glad, because this brother of yours was dead and is alive again; he was lost and is found.' "

Remarks:

The son who left his father's house is an example of the souls who forsake God and His house. That son went to a far off country where he wasted his inheritance in immoral living. When he spent it all, he began to be in need. So he worked feeding the swine and he longed to fill his belly with the pods that the swine did eat.

All this gives us a picture as to what sin and living away from God might lead to. But as soon as that son felt how bad his situation was, he arose and came to his father asking forgiveness. This parable shows us the steps toward repentance. The Lord Jesus said regarding that son, "He arose and came to his father. But when he was yet a great way off, his father saw him and had compassion and ran and fell on his neck and kissed him." Luke 15:20.

How strong these words are and how explicit this illustration is by which the Lord Jesus wanted to show His great love and compassion to backsliders.

"But when he was a great way off." What do these words show us except yearning and waiting? I am sure the father probably looked out several times a day to see if his son was returning. That is why he saw his son returning even when his son was far off. Oh, how God the Father loves you and desires so greatly for you to return to Him. The earthly father, emotionally moved, waits for his son who had forsaken him and went out to do many sins. If this is the case with the earthly father whose life is full of weaknesses, how much then of the feelings of the Heavenly Father toward those who have backslid?

Jesus told us about God's love and His desire to be good to us in another part of the Bible saying, "If ye, then, being evil, know how to give good gifts unto your children, how much more shall your Father which is in Heaven give good things to those that ask Him?" Matthew 7:11.

What was the reaction of the father upon seeing his lost son? "He had compassion and ran and fell on his neck and kissed him." The father had proceeded with all these steps toward his son even before the son uttered one word. That the son was turning back to the father showed to the father that this previously wayward son was truly humbling himself and truly wanted to make things right. And notice that the returning son was not seeking or demanding any rights. He was merely seeking forgiveness and the chance to now truly obey his father if only as a servant - not even with full privileges as a son.

The father's compassion for his son just overtook the father. The father could not contain himself. He had to celebrate the returning of his son. That is love which forgives and truly forgets all sins. If the physical father showed that great love toward his sinful son, how much greater is God's love toward the prodigal ones who sincerely turn back to Him. In spite of the sins of the backslider - which fully deserve eternal punishment in Hell - God will immediately forgive the truly repentant just as He promises and so longs to do.

God has compassion upon them and desires so intensely to free them from their slavery? He is the One Who said, "They that be whole need not a physician, but they that are sick. I am not come to call the righteous, but sinners to repentance." Matthew 9:12-13.

The father experienced all these feelings for his son, but how did the son act toward his father? While the son was in the far off country, he promised himself to apologize to his father, saying, "Father, I have sinned against Heaven and before thee and am no worthy to be called your son, make me as one of your hired servants.", Luke 15:18-19, However, it happened that when he met his father, he uttered those words but the father did not let him say the last sentence which is, "Make me as one of your hired servants." This behavior on the part of the father has a very important significance in our relationship with God. When we sincerely repent, God reinstates us as sons. Jesus paid with His Holy Blood as price for this sonship. "For as much as ye know that ye were not redeemed with corruptible things, as silver and gold from your vain conversation, received by tradition from your fathers. But with the precious blood of Christ as of a lamb without blemish and without spot.", 1 Peter 1:18-19, The expression "Our Father" is a beautiful one which the Lord rejoices in hearing. That is why He asked His disciples to use it. "When you pray, say, 'Our Father, Who art in Heaven.'" Luke 11:2.

In this parable, what happened after the lost son apologized and repented? The father ordered his servants to "Bring forth the best robe and put it on him and put a ring on his hand and shoes on his feet. And bring hither the fatted calf and kill it and let us be merry. For this my son was dead and is alive again; he was lost and is found." Luke 15:22-24.

The son became naked by sinning and the father put clothes on him - the best robe He had. This is what repentance does, it puts robes of righteousness on the sinner. Robes that were bought by the precious Blood of Jesus. We might wonder and ask ourselves, Doesn't the older son, who spent his life obeying his father, deserve all that? But this is the compassion of the father, for the father pities the sick son more than the rest of his brothers. Also, the Heavenly Father pities the spiritually sick more than the ninety-nine who did not need a doctor.

The ring which was put on his hand is a sign of the covenant between the father and his son. He does not remember his sins anymore. All that the father cared to do was to cover his son's nakedness so that he might look like a son again, as if he had not done any evil. All that the son offered his father was his heartfelt repentance and a true willingness to obey from that point on, even as a servant. But the father rewarded him with all his blessings. Likewise in our relationship with our Heavenly Father, we need only offer Him our sincere repentance and a true willingness to obey from that point on, and He will accept us and give us of His abundant richness and spiritual gifts to re-establish the blessings that were lost by sinning.

My reader, look at God's great mercy and His love and compassion to you and His eagerness to re-establish you to salvation. Even though you have disobeyed Him and turned your back to Him, truly repent from your heart and ask God to forgive you by praying as follows:

(Prayer on next page.)

Prayer To Repent And Come Back To Jesus:

"Lord Jesus, I realize I have turned my back to you. But now I turn back to You, Lord Jesus. Come back into my heart and forgive me of all my sins. Wash me in Your Blood, and make me clean again. I have sinned against Heaven and before You and am not worthy to be called a son. I receive You again by faith as my Lord and Savior.

I also realize that Lordship means that I commit from my heart to willingly obey You in all things. As I repent and confess my sin I know you are faithful and just to forgive me of all sin and to cleanse me from all unrighteousness. This you promise in your Word. I know I don't deserve Your mercy but I know you are merciful to me because You are faithful to Your Word. Jesus, cover me in Your precious Blood. Lord, I commit never to profane your Blood ever again. And I know in your strength that I can overcome. Lord, I no longer want to sin against you.

Thank you Jesus for forgiving me."

CHAPTER 10

HOW TO OVERCOME SIN AND TEMPTATION

The best sermons that I know of that will help you overcome sin and temptation are the temptation sermons by Keith Moore.

http://www.moorelife.org

Click on "Free Downloads/Word Supply"

Enter Search Phrase: temptation

They are the most practical and effective teachings that I know of that will actually help you to overcome all sin. I greatly urge you to keep listening to these sermons over and over and over again until you have completely overcome all sin. At the same time keep asking God to create in you a clean heart. Remember your eternal life is at stake.

These sermons can also be freely downloaded as MP3 files from:

http://www.mediafire.com/file/jbs88sw7rg85bfb/0903-Temptation-00.mp3

http://www.mediafire.com/file/bysj2477q7dubvh/0903-Temptation-06.mp3

http://www.mediafire.com/file/1wwrkta98h5sr7l/0903-Temptation-07.mp3

http://www.mediafire.com/file/ipa3upxma5ktszn/0903-Temptation-08.mp3

http://www.mediafire.com/file/4a2vvj4x1qgjtig/0903-Temptation-09.mp3

ABOUT THE AUTHOR

Mike Peralta was born in Phoenix, Arizona. He received Jesus Christ as his Lord and Savior in 1979. He is a graduate of the University of Arizona in Tucson, Arizona. He has worked in the Electronic and Semiconductor Industry since 1982. He is currently working as a Semiconductor Device Modeling Engineer in Phoenix, Arizona.

His email is at: peralta_mike@hotmail.com

His website is at: hell3.weebly.com
This website has many testimonies of Hell
and of the very soon rapture of the true saints.

Other Books By Mike Peralta:

Hell Testimonies
This book (434 pages) has many revelations of Hell that God has given to various people around the world. These messages should be taken very seriously. There are many, many people in Hell right now that thought they were right with God but they found out at the moment of their death that they were not, because of sin and disobedience in their lives, and then they found themselves in Hell. Because of this it is eternally vital that you read these testimonies of Hell and to repent of any and all sins.

Keep A Look Out For Soon To Be Published Books. Look at Amazon.com and Smashwords.com

Time is very short and I am endeavoring to be sensitive to the Holy Spirit about what books to publish.

Keep getting closer and closer to Jesus, keep reading His Word, and keep obeying all His commandments written and spoken.